Psychology in the Justice System

Jared A. Linebach, Ph.D.

Lea M. Kovacsiss, Ph.D.

Front Cover Image: Floyd County Superior Court, Rome, GA

DEDICATION

I dedicate this work to my students who have help shape its content and to
the practitioners who live in these areas daily.
Thank you!! ~JL

I dedicate this work to my parents who nurtured my interest in forensic
psychology and supported my academic journey. ~LK

CONTENTS

ACKNOWLEDGMENTS

A special thanks needs to be extended to Debra Bekerian and Peter English, my graduate mentors, who tirelessly shaped my love of the application of psychology within the justice system. This work would not have been possible without the encouragement of my wife, Katy; thank you for your never-ending support of my goals. Similarly, this work would not have been possible without the detailed, editing eye of my good friend and brother, Mark Hanigan.

-JL

Thank you to Steven Hurwitz and Elizabeth Athaide-Victor for sharing their passion of forensic psychology and for serving as mentors inside and outside of the classroom. I have greatly appreciated the opportunity to learn from you. Also, thank you to Mark Hanigan for his detailed and thoughtful edits and suggestions.

-LK

1 INTRODUCTION

The purpose of this book is to introduce aspects of forensic psychology that the reader may not realize are relevant to this field. Forensic psychology can be broadly defined as any area of the legal system where psychology is applied or consulted. This broad definition is integral to the book's foundation as seemingly disjointed topics are weaved together under the overarching umbrella of forensic psychology.

When one thinks about the utilization of psychology in the legal system, thinking most often begins with some concept of criminal profiling. While profiling criminals is an aspect of forensic psychology, it is only a small portion. Within forensic psychology, there are two distinct areas in which forensic psychologists operate. The two vastly different areas are as follows:

- **Practical/Clinical**: focuses on the ever-present needs of individuals in the legal system.
- **Research**: focuses on gathering and compiling data in a useful manner.

Clinicians focus on populations close to the legal system such as jail or prison inmates, correctional officers, and police officers. Researchers may also focus on populations close to the legal system, but are not limited to those individuals. Researchers may, for example, be interested in the public's perception of a proposed new law or how closely a constituency agrees with a sheriff's stances on certain issues.

While both of these areas are important, the purpose of this book is not to explore the distinctions between them. Herein, you will find topics relevant to forensic psychology in the broad sense, but still related to its major subfields, including the following:

- Criminal psychology

- Police and investigative psychology
- Correctional psychology
- Legal psychology
- Victimology

Criminal psychology deals with the psychological reasons why criminals commit the crimes they commit and behave in the ways they behave. Police and investigative psychology addresses the psychological well-being and trauma that accompanies being involved in law enforcement activities, either as a criminal or as a police officer. Correctional psychology focuses on well-being and trauma that accompanies participating in a correctional facility either as a criminal or a correctional officer. Legal psychology concentrates on the psychological repercussions of laws and being involved in the legal process. Victimology, from the standpoint of forensic psychology, is interested in the psychological well-being and trauma associated with being victimized.

Clearly, this text is not exhaustive; however, it provides the reader with a sampling of topics and examples of psychology being used within and regarding the legal system.

Each chapter in this text falls into at least one of the major subfields. Criminal psychology is discussed in Chapters 2 and 3. Police psychology is addressed in Chapters 4, 6, and 9. Investigative psychology is considered in Chapter 12. Correctional psychology is described within Chapters 7 and 10. Legal psychology is discussed in Chapters 8 and 11. Victimology is covered by Chapters 5, 13, and 14.

Chapter 2 begins with an exploration of the work of two theorists related to the field of forensic psychology. The two theorists discussed in Chapter 2 attempted to describe or profile criminals in their day. Cesare Lombroso attempted to explain criminal activity as a result of biological abnormalities while Gabriel Tarde attempted to explain criminal activity as a result of imitation.

Chapter 3 addresses some of the aspects of social learning theory as it applies to aggression and to the development of juvenile delinquency. The psychological theory or social learning is applied to aggression and delinquency in this chapter. The impact of social learning theory is also discussed as it relates to the juvenile justice system.

Chapter 4 examines the history of police civil liability since the addition of Section 1983 of the Civil Rights Act. Though Section 1983 allows violation-of-rights suits to be brought against any member of the government, most of the suits are brought against members of the law enforcement community. This dramatic increase in suits brought against law enforcement personnel has resulted in an increased focus on risk management to reduce the impact of civil liability cases.

Chapter 5 addresses the disparities between all sex workers versus those who are forced to work as sex workers. The chapter considers the differences between individuals who engage in prostitution of their own free will and those who are forced into the profession through human trafficking and the sex trade. This chapter also discusses the psychological trauma associated with human trafficking and forced prostitution.

Chapter 6 discusses police stress and its extreme – traumatic stress. For centuries, police officers have been dealing with the stress associated with their line of work. This, however, has not made coping with the stress any easier. Officers who are involved in traumatic situations for which they are ill-equipped may fall prey to traumatic stress or Post-Traumatic Stress Disorder (PTSD). Factors that may contribute to the development of PTSD are considered.

Chapter 7 scrutinizes California's summary parole initiative along with its impact to the community and mental health professionals. The summary parole initiative allows inmates who committed non-serious and non-violent crimes to be released from prison up to 20 months early with very little, if any, supervision. This, in turn, places an increased burden on community services, including mental health services.

Chapter 8 analyzes decision making on the part of judicial actors in the criminal justice system. Models of decision making are proposed and dissected for their applicability to judicial decision making.

Chapter 9 considers the possible constitutional dilemmas related to video policing. Video policing can be effective as a force multiplier, but can also have serious civil liberties implications. Though a feature called pixilation is used to respect the privacy of individual citizens, some groups, such the American Civil Liberties Union (ACLU), are still concerned that those precautions will not be sufficient to address all privacy concerns.

Chapter 10 reviews the development of modern sex offender management policies. California's *Sexually Violent Predator Act* (1995) is analyzed in the context of preceding legislation along with the U.S. Supreme Court's decision in *Kansas v. Hendricks*. The civil commitment of sexual offenders is compared to both other civil sanctions and the U.S. Supreme Court's decision in *U.S. v. Halper*.

Chapter 11 takes a hard look at lethal injection, addressing some apparent behavioral assumptions related to this specific form of the death penalty. Behavioral assumptions include the use of drugs for humans that are not approved for domesticated-animal euthanasia, the theory of three drugs being "better than one", and the assumption that those individuals administering the three-drug cocktail know what they are doing and are properly trained to administer such drugs.

Chapter 12 discusses the use of hypnosis in the criminal justice system. Many cases have attempted to specify when and how forensic hypnosis should be utilized. Unfortunately, even when hypnosis has been admissible in court, there have been some cases of adverse side effects to the person undergoing hypnosis. These adverse side effects have resulted in several states adopting strict guidelines for the use of forensic hypnosis cleverly rebranded as "focused meditation".

Chapter 13 is an evaluation of a legal decision made by the U.S. Supreme Court. When a child enters the office of a school official and is told that their conversations will be kept confidential, it is not often that the child will question that official's sincerity. Frequently, a child will accept what he or she is being told wholeheartedly. Such was the situation with Jeffery Woodard, a student at a Bible-centered, private school in Florida. Mr. Todd Bellhorn, one of Jupiter Christian School's employees, was asked to counsel Woodard in regard to his sexual orientation. According to testimony by Woodard, only after receiving spoken assurance that the conversation would remain confidential did he admit his homosexuality. However, confidentiality was not kept at all.

Chapter 14 takes a look at intimate partner violence against males. Men are more likely to be victimized by strangers, but when they are victimized by intimate partners, they tend to experience more serious forms of violence. While intimate partner violence can include men and women from heterosexual and homosexual relationships, this review focuses on male victimizations perpetrated by female intimate partners. Researchers have debated the true rate of male victimization by intimate partners for years; some believe rates are consistently underreported and Western patriarchal traditions contribute to underreporting. Others believe over-emphasis on male victimizations in intimate relationships is nothing more than "feminist backlash," distracting from the overwhelming prevalence of female victimization by men. The goal of this chapter is to consider male victimization and the barriers to accessing social services that might be needed by these victims.

2 AN INTRODUCTION TO CRIME

Every theory about crime and delinquency ever conjured has had its supporters and its critics. Most criminological theories are controversial, and none are flawless, nor do they explain all criminality perfectly. Some examples of an inability to explain all criminality include the classical school of criminology, positivist school of criminology, biological trait theories, and psychological trait theories. The classical school explained crime as solely a manifestation of free will; however, it failed to consider other aspects of the individual, such as one's upbringing or genetics. The positivist school explained crime as a manifestation of the characteristics of the individual that cannot be controlled by the individual. In other words, the positivist school completely removed the concept of free will from the cause of crime. The biological trait and psychological trait theories focused on their respective disciplines to the complete exclusion, in most cases, of other disciplines. However, there are segments of each theory that can be applied reasonably to many aspects of behavior.

Gabriel Tarde and Cesare Lombroso represent two classic theories whose underlying ideas have clashed in the past. Tarde was wholly convinced of the behavioral side of delinquency, while Lombroso was equally committed to the biological factors contributing to delinquency. The theorists were quite successful at developing their respective theories; therefore, a comparison of their contributions to the field will be analyzed to assess the applicability of the strengths of each respective theory.

Gabriel Tarde's Commitment to Behavior

First, an analysis of Gabriel Tarde and his theory of Imitation of Diffusion in Society is appropriate. Tarde, a French criminologist and sociologist, probably could be considered a theorist who went against the grain since, during his career, the majority of prominent theories were

5

falling into the category focusing on biological causes (Vold, Bernard, & Snipes, 1998). The foundational precepts of Tarde's theory of Imitation of Diffusion in Society flew squarely in the faces of those holding a biological perspective because they took into account only the psychological factors that contribute to criminal behavior. However, "Tarde rejected Lombroso's theory that crime was caused by biological abnormality, arguing that criminals were primarily normal people who, by accident of birth, were brought up in an atmosphere in which they learned crime as a way of life" (Vold, Bernard, & Snipes, 1998). Tarde took his knowledge base of one way in which people can learn, and applied it to the forensic population.

Though Tarde wrote several books on the subject of imitation, the ideas were not original with him. He borrowed ideas from European anthropologists who had originally presented such ideas of imitation applied in the social sciences (Kinnunen, 1996). However, Tarde began his exhibition with a phenomenon produced when large crowds of people gather together in one place. Tarde looked at crowds in general, but he also considered the interactions between family members (Borch, 2005; Borch, 2006). Borch (2005) points out that imitation typically occurs as an inferior member of a group or family observes and mimics the behaviors of a superior member of the same group or family. Illustrated, the children in a household imitate the father, and members of an organization imitate the leader (Brasol, 1927). These correlations make sense, and are supported by social-learning concepts (Mihalic & Elliott, 1997), since when an individual is unsure of group expectations, he or she will study another individual who possesses knowledge of the perceived expectations.

Tarde's "laws of imitation" are threefold:

- The first law purported by Tarde suggests that the degree to which an individual imitates another is directly related to the amount of time exposed to that individual.
- The second law formally states the above-stated principle: that the superior member is mimicked by the inferior member.
- The third law proposes that old habits or ways of doing something are replaced by newer ways or habits, implying a constant change in the imitated behavior (Vold, Bernard, & Snipes, 1998).

Having the laws spelled out makes it much easier to understand them and to examine each of them more closely. It should be mentioned that "Tarde's views were not widely disseminated outside France" (Hibbert, 1963).

Research has been conducted that illustrates the first law stated by Tarde. A phenomenon studied and named "social implosion" by Rodney Stark and William Bainbridge considers an intense pull for the attention of a new member of a cult (Myers, 2002). The members of the cult essentially cut the new member off from any other views that differed from those of the cult. It was the desire of the cult members to create what Tarde called a "social repetition to somnambulism or hypnosis" (Borch, 2005, p. 83). Furthermore, Borch (2012) points out that "crowd members follow the norms of the group not because of contagious suggestion, but because of an extensive pressure towards conformity" (p. 253). It seems as though it was Tarde's conviction that people, criminals in particular, were walking around as zombies, simply watching others and copying what they saw.

In Tarde's second law of imitation, he unashamedly focuses on the hierarchical structures found within groups. Bonds that tie individuals to a particular social group are a natural condition. The bond leads the individual, sometimes unconsciously, to imitate, follow and adhere to the norms of living established in and practiced by the community (Brasol, 1927). It is the influence of the senior members of a group that keeps the junior members focused on the beliefs of the organization of which they are a part. Brasol (1927), while speaking of the influence that a superior individual has on an inferior individual, indicates that the inferior individual is most impacted by the habits, thoughts, words, principles, and convictions of the superior individual.

Tarde had to provide room in his theory for changes and adaptations in criminal activity that were prevalent then and now. The third law does not deny, but rather promotes and expects changes in criminal patterns and advances. In the example of the family, the child imitates the parents due to what he/she perceives to be right because it is being perpetuated by father and mother (Brasol, 1927). However, with the mental development that occurs in the child's mind, there are substantial adaptations that are produced in the growing child (Brasol, 1927). Obviously, there is always room for improvement, especially when law enforcement catches up with the criminal. Therefore, there will always be some individuals who take it upon themselves to invent new deviant behaviors and teach them to individuals less inclined to think for themselves. Ultimately, it can be said of Tarde that he succeeded in stressing the importance of social factors in the causation of crime (Hibbert, 1963). Tarde's theories may not have made it beyond the borders of Europe, but he influenced others to at least consider the implications of imitation.

Cesare Lombroso's Commitment to Biology

Conversely, Cesare Lombroso in Italy was developing his own theory of crime. His was centered on biological causes rather than behavioral ones. Lombroso's training was in the fields of medicine and eventually psychiatry. Therefore, his theory based on strictly biological causes is a logical move for him (Vold, Bernard, & Snipes, 1998). The foundational tenant of Lombroso's theory was his belief in atavism or the idea that criminals were biological throwbacks, people more primitive and less highly evolved than noncriminal people (Vold, Bernard, & Snipes, 1998). Borrowing heavily from the work of Charles Darwin, Lombroso believed that a criminal could be classified as a murderer by the slant of his forehead or classified as a sexual offender by the fullness of his or her lips (Wilson & Herrnstein, 1985). For Lombroso, physical characteristics were the only causal factors of criminal behavior that were worth analyzing.

Klempner and Parker (1981) summarize Lombroso's theory into four segments:

- First, each of those who are prone to crime has a physical type that is distinctive and noticeable from his or her birth.
- Second, those who are prone to crime can be recognized by those distinctive characteristics.
- Third, it emphasizes the notion that causality cannot be drawn from these characteristics, but rather aid in the identification of those who would be more prone to certain crimes.
- Fourth, it maintains that the method of intervention for these individuals is relentless socialization.

The summary presented by Klempner and Parker (1981) is most beneficial to a critical analysis of the theory.

The first segment of Lombroso's theory asserts that, from birth, some individuals are predestined to become criminals; there is little to be done to reverse that fact. Despite Lombroso's assertion that the behavior of the criminal was predestined for the individual from birth, he also recognized that an individual's experiences may or may not cause those behaviors to be present in the individual (Wilson & Herrnstein, 1985). Even though Lombroso held that criminals are predestined to conform to delinquent behavior from birth, he had little evidence to substantiate his claims.

The second segment of his theory was what he spent the majority of his time working on and perfecting. Due to his education in medicine, he was primarily concerned with the physical properties – including those of the brain – that made a criminal a criminal. Lombroso's perspective is summed up by Klempner & Parker (1981): the habitual criminal is essentially made up of an anatomical, physiological, psychological and social stigmatized set of human characteristics. It was the belief of Lombroso that the criminal was less evolved or developed than the typical human being. Lombroso's methods of gathering information for his book were autopsies of dead criminals and assessments of the physical characteristics of living criminals. However, he never tested his theories by comparing criminals' characteristics to those of non-criminals (Klempner & Parker, 1981; Vold, Bernard, & Snipes, 1998). Lombroso, along with many others, examined the entirety of his subjects' bodies to ensure that nothing was overlooked; so much so that he was unsurpassed by the professionals of his time in his care for and thoroughness of his subjects (Hibbert, 1963). Despite the controversy of his theory, his methodology and practice of assessing the characteristics in which he was interested was paramount.

Lombroso's concern for the appropriate causality is intriguing. He maintained that causality could not be drawn from the physical characteristics themselves. However, they were merely predetermined factors in the identification of criminals. Lombroso eventually conceded that society was responsible for more crime than was evolutionary atavism (Wilson & Herrnstein, 1985). The fact of the matter is that Lombroso was bent on the biological factors being the crucial pivot point on which the criminal activity or behavior hinges.

It is quite interesting, in considering the final segment, that Lombroso would consider a behavioral solution to a biological problem. He concludes that the method of intervention for the individual to overcome his or her desires of criminal activity is to engage one's self in a large amount of social interaction. Lombroso's ideas were somewhat primitive, considering that the limits to the biological knowledge of his time were significantly different from the limits of today. However, Lombroso did not consider biological remedies to the situations posed by the population in which he was interested. The preferred method of intervention for inmates was rehabilitation rather than retribution (Wilson & Herrnstein, 1985). The preferred method involved a psychological effort as opposed to a physical or biological alternative. Quite possibly, Lombroso's dedication and passion for his theory pushed him beyond reason and even beyond the ability to analyze his theory objectively, based on inconsistencies between the perceived problem and the assumed most-beneficial intervention.

Conclusion

Though these two theorists have opposing viewpoints, neither of them is completely correct nor completely incorrect. Each one has its strengths and weaknesses. The opposition that each one received served to be somewhat beneficial. Tarde seemed to have a better developed analysis of the available data than Lombroso, but had limited means of testing his theory. Similarly, Lombroso had ample means of testing his theory, but was slightly further off base when it came to actually solving the problem of the cause of criminal activity. Despite the inconsistencies between the two, it is most probable that some form of a combination of these two theories would have fared the test of time much better.

Questions for Discussion

1. a. How are the theories of Tarde and Lombroso different? b. How are they similar?

2. How did Tarde's laws of imitation contribute to his theory?
3. a. What is the foundation for Tarde's theory? b. What is the foundation for Lombroso's theory?
4. How have current theories of crime changed since Tarde and Lombroso?
5. Are we still using similar spin-offs of these early theorists or are current theories completely novel and revolutionary?

References

Borch, C. (2005). Urban imitations: Tarde's sociology revisited. *Theory, Culture & Society, 22*(3), 81-100.

Borch, C. (2006). The exclusion of the crowd: The destiny of a sociological figure of the irrational. *European Journal of Social Theory, 9*(1), 83-102.

Borch, C. (2012). *The politics of crowds: An alternative history of sociology.* New York: Cambridge University Press.

Brasol, B. (1927). *The elements of crime (psycho-social interpretation).* New York: Oxford University Press.

Hibbert, C. (1963). *The roots of evil: A social history of crime and punishment.* Boston, MA: Little, Brown and Company.

Kinnunen, J. (1996). Gabriel Tarde as a founding father of innovation diffusion research. *Acta Sociologica, 39*, 431-442.

Klempner, J. and Parker, R. D. (1981). *Juvenile delinquency and juvenile justice.* New York: Franklin Watts.

Mihalic, S. W. & Elliott, D. (1997). A social learning theory model of marital violence. *Journal of Family Violence, 12*(1), 21-47.

Myers, D. G. (2002). *Social psychology (7th Ed.).* Boston, MA: McGraw-Hill Companies, Inc.

Vold, G. B., Bernard, T. J., & Snipes, J. B. (1998). *Theoretical criminology, (4th Ed.).* New York: Oxford University Press.

Wilson, J. Q. and Herrnstein, R. J. (1985). *Crime and human nature.* New York: Simon & Schuster, Inc.

3 THE APPLICATION OF SOCIAL LEARNING THEORY TO THE PSYCHOLOGY OF CRIME

Social learning theory is a psychological theory that gleans concepts from behaviorism and learning theory (Brauer & Tittle, 2012). Social learning theory is a theory of integration whereby people, especially children, learn things from watching other people. The architects of this theory reason that people learn things

- from watching one another,
- from listening to one another, and
- from taking cues from one another (Brauer & Tittle, 2012).

Young girls learn appropriate behaviors from their mothers and older females, while young boys learn appropriate behaviors from their fathers and older males (Barclay, 1982). Additionally, we learn from our peer groups, teachers, and those in the media. "Moreover, recent formulations of social learning theory suggest that learning occurs through both direct and vicarious behavioral reinforcement" (Brauer & Tittle, 2012, p. 159). With the advancement of technology, no longer does one who does the reinforcing need to be a tangible presence in the life of the learner.

Just as people will learn socially acceptable behaviors from those around them, they will also learn socially inappropriate behaviors from those with whom they come in contact. Socially unacceptable behaviors are those which are contrary to cultural norms, but are not necessarily deviant or criminal. The concept of reinforcement is a large part of the motivation behind a specified behavior. Reinforcement may be used to elicit socially unacceptable behavior just the same as it can elicit deviant behavior (Brauer & Tittle, 2012). Reinforcement becomes the driving force or motivator when it is greater than the corresponding punishment for the deviant behavior.

Social Learning and Aggression

One of the easiest ways to learn how to perform a task is by watching some other knowledgeable person perform that task, which is essentially the premise of Social Learning Theory. Many theories are present in society that suggest just how victims of crime become victims. Social Learning Theory is one that has received much notoriety from victimologists. Victimization as a result of social learning begins long before any actual victimization occurs. It is asserted that children who watch parents or older siblings victimize will, in turn, commit criminal activity themselves (Waddell, Lipman, & Offord, 1999).

Since, for the first four or five years of a child's life, he or she is learning almost completely from the parents, it makes sense that the confines of a family unit would provide the best training ground. The family is able to teach violence, techniques of violence, and approval of violence (Mihalic & Elliott, 1997). With all of this violence being propagated, there must be a victim within the family who is the object of all such aggression. Forsstrom & Rosenbaum (1985) proposed that

> [S]eeing one's mother in a helpless situation transmits the message that women are helpless to control their own lives, thus promoting depression in female children, who would be most likely to identify with the victim/mother. Men witnessing parental conjugal violence might be more likely to identify with the aggressor/father rather than with the victim, thus avoiding depression. (p. 470)

The family history of abuse can contribute to an elevated level of victimization (Chen, Thrane, Whitbeck, Johnson, & Hoyt, 2007). This merely adds to the propensity for an individual to acquire the traits necessary to be afforded the diagnosis of conduct disorder later in life.

In the study conducted by Mihalic & Elliott (1997), repeated victimization was found to be an indicator and "important learning mechanism" for later victimization and aggression (p. 42). This, however, was only the case with males. Females followed a slightly different path. "Females, with their more nurturing personalities, may have stronger emotional reactions to […] violence, thus impacting their lives to a more significant degree" (Mihalic & Elliott, 1997, p. 43). The study neglected to elaborate on how their lives are impacted based on this finding of greater significance. Similarly, it was proposed that violence is "more visible to females, since they often spend more time at home than males, especially at younger ages" (Mihalic & Elliott, 1997, p. 43-44). Gender differentiation is inconclusive in its assessment of aggression and victimization later in the individual's life. "If strategies for aggression and conflict resolution are learned, not innate, then women are likely to learn different methods than men" (Björkqvist, 1994, p. 178). Just because women are likely to learn different methods of aggression does not mean that aggression needs to be learned at all. If aggression is learned, it can be controlled or unlearned.

Conduct Disorder and Delinquency

Conduct disorder is a product of aggression (Schaeffer, Petras, Ialongo, Poduska, & Kellam, 2003). "The main ingredients of [conduct disorder] are aggression, antisocial behavior, academic failure, […], abuse and criminality" (Olsson, Hansson, & Cederblad, 2008, p. 121). Schaeffer and colleagues (2003) found that aggressive behavior significantly predicted the development of antisocial outcomes – namely delinquency, conduct disorder and antisocial personality disorder. Aggression and its subsequent antisocial outcomes place an economic burden on society (Romeo, Knapp, & Scott, 2006). Foster and Jones (2005) found that the expenses paid by government assistance programs for individuals with conduct disorder were $70,000 more per year than those classified as impaired but not with conduct disorder.

Some of the costs associated with conduct disorder are the costs of interaction with law enforcement. Conduct disorder, by its very nature, lends itself to be the catch-all diagnosis for children who come into negative contact with the law. However, "not all youths with conduct disorder have a criminal record, and not all youths with a criminal record have conduct disorder" (Bassarath, 2001, p. 610). The relationships between negative interaction with law enforcement, delinquency, and disorder generally are not distinguished easily by non-professionals (Wakefield, Kirk, Pottick, Hsieh, & Tian, 2006). Wakefield and colleagues (2006) found that lay persons decided to classify some individuals as without a conduct disorder, when they, in fact, qualified under the Diagnostic and Statistical Manual's (DSM) criteria. This, then, requires a closer cross-reference look at the relationships between those with and without a diagnosable conduct disorder and those who do and do not interact negatively with law enforcement.

Diagnosable conduct disorder is a disorder of adolescence where the propensity for antisocial tendencies arises earlier in childhood (Clarizio, 1997). There are four main areas that are taken into account when a diagnosis of conduct disorder is considered:

- Aggression
- Destruction of property
- Lying or theft
- Serious violation of rules (Clarizio, 1997)

All of these areas, and their corresponding subareas, are closely related to the reasons an adolescent would come into contact with law enforcement, making his or her behavior delinquent.

Since conduct disorder behaviors do not commence "overnight", there are contributing risk factors that undoubtedly can be observed. Factors that are both within the individual's control and not within the individual's control contribute to the development of conduct disorder. These risk factors include individual factors such as age, gender, Attention-Deficit Hyperactivity Disorder (ADHD), impulse-control issues, temperament, aggression, depression, and academic underachievement (Clarizio, 1997; Holmes, Slaughter, & Kashani, 2001).

Additional risk factors are psychosocial and environmental, genetic and nutritional, and neurological (Holmes et al., 2001). Psychosocial and environmental factors that contribute to conduct disorder are lower educational- and occupational-levels of one's father and living with a single parent or relative (Al-Banna, Al-Bedwawi, Al-Saadi, Al-Maskari, & Eapen, 2008). Genetic and nutritional factors refer to the biological predisposition established by the individual's family and the level of nutrition experienced during childhood. Similarly, neurological deficits were obvious in a study conducted by Olvera, Semrud-Clikeman, Pliszka, & O'Donnell, 2005). The deficits observed by Olvera and colleagues (2005) included verbal impairments, executive-functioning impairments and visual integration and facial-recognition impairments.

Implications for the Juvenile Justice System

It is true that a burden falls on the juvenile justice system to maintain order within the juvenile population. Fortunately, with the rise of conduct disorder prevalence in the juvenile justice system, there has not been a corresponding increase in stigmatism regarding mental illness in juvenile courts (Murrie, Boccaccini, McCoy, & Cornell, 2007). Murrie and colleagues (2007) found that the most common method of handling juveniles with documented psychopathy or conduct disorder was referral out to a capable mental facility. Even though this mode is being employed, there are still gaps and differences between jurisdictions (Murrie et al., 2007).

There is a belief that juvenile justice might be better served in a government treatment-program rather than in a government institution behind bars. Several studies have been conducted that concluded that the best method of rehabilitation is to create better, more cost-effective programs for juvenile offenders (Al-Banna et al., 2008; Chen et al., 2007; Foster & Jones, 2005). The consensus of Foster and Jones (2005) regarding the reallocation of funding is that money should be taken from dealing with problem behaviors and spent on preventing those behaviors. Similarly, Al-Banna and colleagues (2008) contend that evidence-based interventions are the only reasonable means of treatment.

Conclusion

The underlying principles of social learning theory can be seen in many aspects of everyday life. Social learning can serve an effective, positive role in society. However, social learning is also used to effect negativity and antisocial behavior in society. When social learning results in negative atmospheres, it can be addressed and reversed. The antisocial behavior must be perceived as such, and there must be a pointed effort, on the part of the one being observed, to change the behavior. With social learning, it is not sufficient to hold to the adage: "do as I say, not as I do."

Questions for Discussion

1. How do males and females differ in their reaction to victimization from childhood to adulthood?
2. From your own experience, are children who witness violence more likely to become victims or criminals when they become adults?
3. a. What are the four main areas taken into account when diagnosing a conduct disorder? b. How can they be seen playing out in the lives of adult offenders?
4. To what extent would juvenile delinquents be served by a merger of a juvenile justice system and a mental health court system?

References

Al-Banna, A., Al-Bedwawi, S., Al-Saadi, A., Al-Maskari, F., & Eapen, V. (2008). Prevalence and correlates of conduct disorder among inmates of juvenile detention centres, United Arab Emirates. *La Revue de Santé de la Méditerranée orientale, 14*(5), 1054-1059.

Barclay, L. (1982). Social learning theory : A framework for discrimination research. *Academy of Management Review, 7*(4), 587-594.

Bassarath, L. (2001). Conduct disorder: A biopsychosocial review. *The Canadian Journal of Psychiatry, 46,* 609-616.

Björkqvist, K. (1994). Sex differences in physical, verbal, and indirect aggression: A review of recent research. *Sex Roles, 30*(3/4), 177-188.

Brauer, J. R. & Tittle, C. R. (2012). Social learning theory and human reinforcement. *Sociological Spectrum: Mid-South Sociological Association, 32*(2), 157-177.

Chen, X., Thrane, L., Whitbeck, L. B., Johnson, K. D., Hoyt, D. R. (2007). Onset of conduct disorder, use of delinquent subsistence strategies, and street victimization among homeless and runaway adolescents in the

Midwest. *Journal of Interpersonal Violence, 22*(9), 1156-1183.

Clarizio, H. F. (1997). Conduct disorder: Developmental considerations. *Psychology in the Schools, 34*(3), 253-265.

Holmes, S. E., Slaughter, J. R., & Kashani, J. (2001). Risk factors in childhood that lead to the development of conduct disorder and antisocial personality disorder. *Child Psychiatry and Human Development, 31*(3), 183-193.

Forsstrom, B. & Rosenbaum, A. (1985). The effects of parental marital violence on young adults: An exploratory investigation. *Journal of Marriage and the Family, May*, 467-472.

Foster, E. M. & Jones, D. E. (2005). The high costs of aggression: Public expenditures resulting from conduct disorder. *American Journal of Public Health, 95*(10), 1767-1772.

Mihalic, S. W. & Elliott, D. (1997). A social learning theory model of marital violence. *Journal of Family Violence, 12*(1), 21-47.

Murrie, D. C., Boccaccini, M. T., McCoy, W., & Cornell, D. G. (2007). Diagnostic labeling in juvenile court: How do descriptions of psychopathy and conduct disorder influence judges? *Journal of Clinical Child and Adolescent Psychology, 36*(2), 228-241.

Olsson, M., Hansson, K., & Cederblad, M. (2008). A follow-up study of adolescents with conduct disorder: Can long-term outcome be predicted from psychiatric assessment data? *Nord Journal of Psychiatry, 62*(2), 121-129.

Olvera, R. L., Semrud-Clikeman, M., Pliszka, S. R., & O'Donnell, L. (2005). Neuropsychological deficits in adolescents with conduct disorder and comorbid bipolar disorder: A pilot study. *Bipolar Disorders, 7*, 57-67.

Romeo, R., Knapp, M., & Scott, S. (2006). Economic costs of severe antisocial behaviour in children – and who pays it. *British Journal of Psychiatry, 188*, 547-553.

Schaeffer, C. M., Petras, H., Ialongo, N., Poduska, J., & Kellam, S. (2003). Modeling growth in boys' aggressive behavior across elementary school: Links to later criminal involvement, conduct disorder, and antisocial personality disorder. *Developmental Psychology, 39*(6), 1020-1035.

Waddell, C., Lipman, E., & Offord, D. (1999). Conduct disorder: Practice, parameters for assessment, treatment, and prevention. *The Canadian Journal of Psychiatry, 44*, 35S-40S.

Wakefield, J. C., Kirk, S. A., Pottick, K. J., Hsieh, D. K., & Tian, X. (2006). The lay concept of conduct disorder: Do nonprofessionals use syndromal symptoms or internal dysfunction to distinguish disorder from delinquency? *The Canadian Journal of Psychiatry, 51*(4), 210-216.

4 POLICE CIVIL LIABILITY

History of Title 42 United States Code § 1983
The history of Section 1983 (42 U.S.C. § 1983) litigation began in the years immediately following the Civil War. In 1866, the United States Congress passed the Civil Rights Act in order to combat the activities of the Ku Klux Klan. Although the Act did not target the Klan specifically, the legislation did establish Federal criminal penalties for state and local government officials who failed to protect the rights of their citizens (Kappeler, Kappeler, & del Carmen, 1993; Means 2004; Ross, 2006; Worrall, 2001). In 1871, Congress added civil penalties through Title 42 United States Code § 1983 to

- redress laws that were unconstitutional;
- allow cases involving constitutional violations to be heard in Federal court, if no options in state courts were available; and,
- allow cases involving constitutional violations to be heard in Federal court in cases where options were technically available in state courts, but they were not being practiced (Kappeler et al., 1993; Ross, 2006, p. 60).

Before, civil cases involving constitutional violations could only be addressed through common law, leaving them in the jurisdictions of the state courts (Ross, 2006). Now, potential litigants had other options.

According to Section 1983:

> Every person who, under color of any statute, ordinance, regulation, custom, or usage, of any State or Territory or the District of Columbia, subjects, or causes to be subjected, any citizen of the United States or other person within the jurisdiction thereof to the deprivation of any rights, privileges, or immunities secured by the Constitution and laws, shall be

liable to the party injured in an action at law, suit in equity, or other proper proceeding for redress […]. (42 U.S.C. § 1983)

The legislation has four important provisions. First, only a protected person can file a suit under Section 1983, meaning the person must be citizen or a person who is governed under the jurisdiction of the United States. Second, the individual or the entity of whom the suit is against must have been acting under the "color of the law," meaning within the scope of official duties. Third, either a person or government entity may be liable. Originally, the words "every person" were narrowly defined by the Supreme Court to mean only individual persons. Since then, new cases have expanded that meaning to include government entities. Finally, and most importantly, in order to bring suit under Section 1983, a constitutional violation must have occurred (Kappeler et al., 1993; Ross, 2006, p. 61). Even though this legislation created an avenue to address both United States Constitutional violations and the state officials who ignored them in Federal court, Section 1983 was sparsely used for 90 years, leaving state tort actions for citizens to handle disputes (Kappeler et al., 1993; Means 2004; Ross, 2006; Worrall, 2001).

Several reasons exist for the failure to successfully bring Section 1983 suits during the decades following the enactment. First, the Ku Klux Klan was an extremely powerful organization with members holding significant government positions, especially in the South. Attempting to sue violators may hardly have seemed worth it to victims – reprisals were a reality and lawsuits took time and money (Means, 2004). Second, interpretation of the statute proved to be difficult. The rights guaranteed by the United States Constitution were narrowly defined by the United States Supreme Court, and, up until the 1950s and 1960s, the Bill of Rights was not actively being applied to the states (Ross, 2006). Third, Section 1983 provided protections against acts committed by officials that were done within the scope of their duties. In many of the cases after the Civil War, acts that were not sanctioned by the government were being committed by officials and caused constitutional violations (Kappeler et al., 1993; Means 2004; Ross, 2006). Section 1983 was not clear as to whether these circumstances warranted state action.

The application of Section 1983 in litigation began changing dramatically with the case of *Monroe v. Pape* (1961). Prior to the *Monroe* ruling, bringing suit against criminal justice professionals was difficult. The U.S. Supreme Court decision broadened the meaning of the statute to include actions of criminal justice professionals who violated constitutional rights while acting under public policy or law. Now, Section 1983 could be used to sue state and local officials who misused their positions of power to violate constitutional rights. Despite the expansion of the meaning of "color of the law," the U.S. Supreme Court continued with its previous interpretation that only individual persons could be sued under Section 1983 and not government entities (Kappeler et al., 1993; Means 2004; Ross, 2006; Worrall, 2001). However, this would change in future litigation.

In the 1970s, two actions would again change the course of Section 1983 litigation. In 1976, the Civil Rights Attorney's Fees Award Act was passed, now known as Section 1988 of Title 42. According to the Act, if a plaintiff prevails in a civil rights lawsuit, the defendant is responsible for the payment of the plaintiff's attorney fees (Means, 2004). In 1978, the U.S. Supreme Court decided *Monell v. Department of Social Services of the City of New York*. In that decision, the U.S. Supreme Court reversed the *Monroe* interpretation that "person" in the statute referred to only individual persons. According to the *Monell* decision, "person" included municipal governments, cities, counties, and their subdivisions (Kappeler et al., 1993; Means, 2004). These two actions in combination would radically change the landscape of police litigation. Before, suing individual persons meant small financial settlements. After *Monell*, plaintiffs could target whole entities with "deep pockets," and, if they prevailed, their attorney fees would be covered.

During this time, Section 1983 suits emerged as the most popular means of seeking actions against law enforcement and remains the most common form of litigation filed against law enforcement personnel. Even though Section 1983 can apply to all government entities and officials, it has impacted law enforcement most significantly (Means, 2004; Ross, 2006; Worrall, 2001). Even when compared to correctional officers and institutions, law enforcement officers are more likely to be sued and to know others within law enforcement who have been sued. Researchers suggest that this trend is due in part to the very nature of law enforcement: Involvement of law enforcement officers is often uninvited, and such involvement can lead to greater threats to life and loss of civil liberties than from other government entities (Hall, Ventura, Lee, & Lambert, 2003).

Standards of Culpability

One of the greatest deficiencies of Section 1983 is the failure to provide concrete standards of culpability for plaintiffs seeking actions. Since no standards exist, the courts have been responsible for defining culpability on a seemingly case-by-case basis. Although some standards have emerged through judicial precedence, standards vary by type of constitutional violation, amendment cited, and jurisdiction. Also, depending on what type of defendant is in an action – supervisor, municipality, department, individual, or some combination thereof – even more possible standards of culpability arise (Amster, 1990; Worrall, 2001). Often, "deliberate indifference" is cited as the common and appropriate standard; however, courts have used much lower standards to define culpability.

In addition to a standard of culpability, the U.S. Supreme Court determined, in *Rizzo v. Goode* (1976), that, in order for supervisors to be found liable in Section 1983 actions, an "affirmative link" must be established between the police misconduct and an adoption of a plan or policy by supervisors that authorized or approved of the conduct (Worrall, 2001). However, no definition of "affirmative link" was offered by the U.S. Supreme Court, which has resulted in numerous interpretations as cases of supervisor liability have been filed. The interpretations are loosely based on three areas: deliberate indifference, knowledge, or negligence (Worrall, 2001). Depending on the court, an affirmative link may be explicitly defined as allowing a constitutional violation to occur. In other instances, an affirmative link may be made in a situation where a supervisor should have known about a constitutional violation.

Standards of municipal liability have been built around two cases: *City of Canton v. Harris* (1989) and *Board of the County Commissioners of Bryan County v. Brown* (1997). The *Canton* case set the standard of deliberate indifference for cases involving failure to train, one of the most common types of claims filed against criminal justice agencies (Ross, 2006; Worrall, 2001). In order for plaintiffs to succeed in proving municipal liability in a failure-to-train suit, they must prove that the government entity in question was deliberately indifferent to the training needs of its employees (King, 2005; Worrall, 2001). Although the *Monell* decision granted liability to government entities, it did not allow vicarious liability, which, by definition, allows for government entities to be responsible for all actions committed by their employees regardless of whether the employer committed a violation. In order to successfully prove government liability for failure to train, the plaintiff must establish a causal connection between the injury and government policy or custom (King, 2005; Means, 2004).

The standard of deliberate indifference is a high standard of culpability and is difficult to prove. As stated in King (2005), "deliberate indifference' is the standard of fault that requires a showing that government policy makers acted with conscious disregard for the obvious consequences of their actions" (p. 23). General court interpretations of deliberate indifference place it somewhere between negligence and purposeful exposure to and knowledge of harm (Justiss, 2009; refer to *Johnston v. Lucas* [1986], *Farmer v. Brennan* [1994], and *Salazar v. City of Chicago* [1991]). Justiss (2009) describes the standard as comparable to criminal intent or recklessness, citing that the courts often require far more than general negligence to prove deliberate indifference. Often, any mitigating effort by the government agency or individual in question is enough to find against deliberate indifference.

A government entity is not automatically liable under Section 1983 for a single incident of deprivation of rights or in the event that an adequate training program was administered incorrectly (King, 2005; Ross, 2006). A plaintiff must prove that the training program in question was grossly inefficient and that the government entities were aware of the situation or should have been aware of the situation. A pattern of violations resulting from the training program in question can be used to meet the deliberate indifference standard. In the absence of a pattern, deliberate indifference can still be proven if government entities continue to rely on a training program that they know, or should have known, could have resulted in violations during trained usage (King, 2005; Ross, 2006). The *Bryan County* case involved the level of culpability necessary to prove liability in negligent hiring. The case resulted from a single incident where the municipality hired an individual with two previous incidents of assault and battery. The Court found that deliberate indifference would again be the appropriate standard for determining culpability (Worrall, 2001). As mentioned previously, several standards of culpability exist, and thorough examination of each is beyond the scope of this brief review. Although deliberate indifference is a stringent standard, officers and administrators must remember that other standards of culpability are less stringent.

Failure to Train

As stated previously, failure to train is one of the most common forms of Section 1983 litigation. The majority of supervisor-liability actions involve failure to train, making it a common area of concern for police administration. Despite the commonality, the deliberate indifference standard is difficult for plaintiffs to meet, and police are victorious in the majority of suits. However, plaintiffs do prevail in failure-to-train litigation in approximately one-third of cases, and, depending on the circumstances, financial awards can be significant (Ross, 2006). The most common police actions are often the most common targets for failure-to-train litigation. They include lethal and non-lethal force, failure to protect, emergency vehicle operations, medical care, arrestee/detainee suicide, and search and seizure (Ross, 2006). Out of all the possible claims against police, claims regarding lethal and non-lethal force are the most successful. Plaintiffs prevail in nearly half of the cases, and they generate the largest monetary awards (Ross, 2006). In order to guard against such suits, departments must provide adequate initial training and refresher training to all officers regarding techniques, proper use of equipment, and any changes in department or judicial policy.

In some circumstances, plaintiffs may prove successfully the unlawful use of force, but such a finding does not automatically support a Section 1983 action for failure to train. In order to ascertain whether a claim is warranted under Section 1983, the courts rely on three principles of

- whether the training program was adequate in preparing officers for circumstances they would encounter while performing their duties;

- whether the training program specifically addressed the matter involved in the suit; and finally,

- if the training program is not adequate in certain areas, whether those specific inadequacies contributed to or caused injury (King, 2005; Ross, 2006, p. 146).

One of the emerging areas of Section 1983 litigation and failure-to-train suits includes law enforcement response to persons with mental illness. Because of the deinstitutionalization of mental illness that began in the 1960s combined with the lack of current community resources, the likelihood that law enforcement officers will encounter persons with mental illness while performing their duties has increased over time. Responding to calls involving persons with mental illness takes a considerable amount of time and department resources (Wells & Schafer, 2006). Researchers have shown that officers will often arrest persons with mental illness, even though they acknowledge such actions are not necessarily appropriate, simply because it is most convenient. In some cases, officers have been known to remove persons with mental illness from their jurisdictions – either by dropping them off in other areas or by practicing "diesel therapy" (i.e., putting the individual on a bus destined for another location) – just to rid themselves of the problem (Wells & Schafer, 2006). Wells and Schafer (2006) found that, even though most departments include dealing with mental illness as part of their general training, officers have indicated a desire for improved training.

The Cost of Litigation

Estimates of the total cost of litigation are difficult to determine. In addition to plaintiffs' awards, agencies must also consider

- the cost of attorney fees, and, in cases where the plaintiffs prevail, plaintiffs' attorney fees;
- out-of-court settlements; and
- the rising cost of liability insurance (Kappeler et al., 1993).

In the early 1980s, researchers estimated the amount of pending litigation at that time could be as high as $780 billion against local governments (Kappeler et al., 1993). In an analysis of 1,359 Section 1983 cases from 1978 through 1990, Kappeler, Kappeler, and del Carmen (1993) found two major increases in the number of cases decided by Federal District Courts: in 1981, the number of cases nearly doubled from the previous year, and in 1985, the number of cases increased approximately 40% from the previous year (p. 331). During the years analyzed, the police prevailed in 52% of the cases, and in cases where liability was found, awards and attorney fees averaged $121,874. Awards ranged from $1 to $1,650,000, depending on the type of claim filed (Kappeler et al., 1993, p. 335).

Ross (2000) conducted a content analysis of 1,525 Section 1983 failure-to-train cases from 1989 to 1999 in order to determine the emerging trends in police liability. The top ten training issues cited in the analysis were non-lethal force (14.8%), false arrest and/or detention (12.1%), search and seizure (11.1%), failure to protect (10.5%), detainee suicide (10%), lethal force (10%), emergency vehicle operations (9.5%), medical care (9%), police as plaintiffs (6.5%), and other (6.4%; Ross, 2000, p. 179). In all of the ten most common areas, the police prevailed in over half of the cases. Plaintiffs were most successful, approximately 42 to 44 percent of the time, in cases involving lethal and non-lethal force, respectively. The largest mean plaintiff awards were in the areas of lethal force and emergency vehicle operations, with both slightly over one million dollars. These two categories also saw the some of the largest mean attorney fees of nearly $100,000. Issues surrounding medical care were also among the top monetary awards, with the mean around $500,000. Attorney fees in this category averaged slightly greater than $100,000. Overall, average plaintiff awards were slightly less than $500,000 with attorney fees around $60,000 (Ross, 2000). Even though the police prevailed in the majority of the cases, awards were significant when they were granted.

Researchers in both studies (Kappeler et al., 1993; Ross, 2000) noted important limitations. Not all litigation cases are published, some are immediately settled out of court, and others are dropped after the initial complaint or early in the litigation process. The data compiled in these studies only provides a glimpse into the litigation cases experienced by police. Actual mean awards and attorney fees could be significantly higher.

When considering both the ever rising costs of attorney fees, for both sides, and potential monetary damages awarded by the courts, some jurisdictions find a financial benefit in out-of-court settlements, regardless of whether the plaintiff has a substantial claim (McCormack, 1994). By settling out of court, police departments may be sending the message that they are guilty of misconduct, when, in fact, their collective reasons were completely financial. In a time when department resources are already strained, defending the integrity of one's department may take a back seat to potential monetary costs. The social implications of such settlements could be significant.

Another component of the potential cost of litigation involves the ability of law enforcement personnel to perform their jobs effectively. In a 2003 study, researchers Hall, Ventura, Lee, & Lambert examined the possibility of police and correction officers developing litigaphobia, the fear of litigation, due to increasing lawsuits and the variables that increased the likelihood of being sued. Approximately half of the officers who participated in the study indicated that they agreed or strongly agreed that the threat of litigation deters potential misconduct. Over half, 62%, of the officers disagreed or strongly disagreed that the threat of litigation impedes their ability to perform duties (Hall et al., 2003). Despite over half of the officers indicating that litigation did not interfere with their ability to perform, the longer an officer was on the job, the more likely he or she was to see litigation as a hindrance to the performance of duties. Further, about half of the officers indicated that threat of civil liability was among the top ten thoughts they had in emergency situations (Hall et al., 2003).

Risk Management

Due to the increasing number of civil-liability claims, many organizations are now under pressure from individuals within their own management or from outside insurance agencies to cut their losses caused by lawsuits. Law enforcement is not exempt from this change. At one time, risk management was a tool for insurance companies; however, within the last 20 years especially, risk management has become a matter of management policy within organizations to decrease the risk of civil liability by

- adapting procedures and techniques that negate risk, and
- continuously training employees of new and emerging areas of potential liability situations (Archbold, 2005; Ross & Bodapati, 2006).

By managing potential risks before a violation occurs, departments potentially save millions in litigation-related costs.

In terms of law enforcement specifically, existing research has suggested that risk managers within police departments are responsible for oversight and management of department policies, training, recruitment and hiring standards, and supervision over line officers. Law enforcement is unique in its ability to use force, and because of that ability, liability claims frequently derive from that area. Liability Assessment and Awareness International (LAAW) suggests that such risk can be managed by careful supervision of line officers, an objective that can be achieved through the following of

- continuous maintenance of department policies and procedures, and
- detailed evaluation of all use of force incidents (Archbold, 2005).

Risk management is more than a response to increasing litigation. With effective risk-management staff, policing agencies can save taxpayer dollars by decreasing the number of lawsuits and payouts. Public and officer safety is increased as officers are continually updated with changes in training protocols and legal mandates. Effective risk management within an organization acknowledges potential issues before they become problems, ensuring a positive working environment for officers, and, in turn, creating positive relationships with the surrounding community.

Conclusion

The United States has a substantial litigious history surrounding government entities and civil rights violations, especially within the last thirty years. Litigation against law enforcement appears to be on the forefront of such actions, accounting for a majority of Section 1983 suits filed. However, plaintiffs are only successful in less than half of the cases. Despite the published odds appearing to be in favor of the police and police administrators, civil litigation is expensive, costing departments millions of dollars every year, not to mention time spent defending allegations and instituting new policies that may result.

Police departments may gain value from training their officers on the circumstances surrounding civil liability in order to prevent such situations from transpiring, but also to help imped the development of litigaphobia among officers – especially among those who have been with the department for some time. Given the increasing number of lawsuits filed every year, the chances of an officer, administrator, or department being named in a civil action has also increased. Law enforcement administrators may benefit from creating risk-management departments within their organizations to help with officer hiring, training, and defending in litigation, as the need arises.

Questions for Discussion

1. Does having cameras or recorders in police vehicles violate a citizen's civil rights?

2. What should be the repercussions for a government official who violates a citizen's civil rights?

3. How would the criminal justice system look today had *Monroe v. Pape* never been decided in a way that reduced the difficulty of bringing lawsuits against government agents?

4. a. How has *Monell v. Department of Social Services of the City of New York* caused citizens whose civil rights have been violated to view state and local government agencies? b. What are the consequences of that view?

References

42 U.S.C. § 1983 (1871).

42 U.S.C. § 1988 (1976).

Amster, R.J. (1990). Note: Defining a uniform culpability standard in Section 1983. *Brooklyn Law Review, 56*, 183-212.

Archbold, C.A. (2005). Managing the bottom line: Risk management in policing. *Policing: An International Journal of Policing Strategies & Management, 28*(1), 30-48. doi: 10.1108/13639510510580968

Board of the County Commissioners of Bryan County, Oklahoma v. Jill Brown et al., 520 U.S. 397 (1997).

City of Canton, Ohio v. Harris et al., 489 U.S. 378 (1989).

Hall, D.E., Ventura, L.A., Lee, Y.H., & Lambert, E. (2003). Suing cops and corrections officers: Officer attitudes and experiences about civil liability. *Policing: An International Journal of Policing Strategies & Management, 26*(4), 529-547. doi: 10.1108/13639510310503505

Justiss, G. (2009). Deliberate indifference under § 1983: Do the courts really care?. *Review of Litigation, 28*(4), 953-981.

Kappeler, V. E., Kappeler, S.F., & del Carmen, R. (1993). A content analysis of police civil liability cases: Decisions of the federal district courts, 1978-1990. *Journal of Criminal Justice, 21*(4), 325-337.

King, M.J. (2005, October). "Deliberate indifference": Liability for failure to train. *FBI Law Enforcement Bulletin, 74*(10), 22-31.

McCormack, W.U. (1994). Attorney's fees in civil litigation. *FBI Law Enforcement Bulletin, 63*(4), 28-32.

Means, R. (2004, May). The history and dynamics of Section 1983. *The Police Chief: The Professional Voice of Law Enforcement, 71*(5). Retrieved from http://policechiefmagazine.org

Monell et al. v. Department of Social Services of the City of New York et al., 436 U.S. 658 (1978).

Monroe at al. v. Pape et al., 365 U.S. 167 (1961).

Rizzo, Mayor of Philadelphia, et al. v. Goode et al., 423 U.S. 362 (1976).

Ross, D.L. (2000). Emerging trends in police failure to train liability: *Policing: An International Journal of Police Strategies & Management, 23*(2), 169-193. doi:10.1108/13639510010333796

Ross, D.L. (2006). *Civil liability in criminal justice.* (4th e.d.). Cincinnati, Ohio: Anderson Publishing.

Ross, D.L. & Bodapati, M.R. (2006). A risk management analysis of the claims, litigation, and losses of Michigan law enforcement agencies: 1985-1999. *Policing: An International Journal of Policing Strategies & Management, 29*(4), 578-601. doi: 10.1108/13639510610648476

Wells, W., & Schafer, J.A. (2006). Officer perceptions of police responses to persons with a mental illness. *Policing: An International Journal of Police Strategies & Management, 29*(4), 578-601. doi:10.1108/12639510610711556

Worrall, J.L. (2001). Culpability standards in Section 1983 litigation against criminal justice officials: When and why mental state matters. *Crime & Delinquency, 47*(1), 28-59.

5 HUMAN TRAFFICKING AND FORCED PROSTITUTION

Human Trafficking: Definitions and Issues
According to the United States Department of State, approximately 600,000 to 800,000 individuals are trafficked internationally every year, and an estimated 14,500 to 17,500 are sent to the United States. Of these hundreds of thousands of victims, 80 percent are female and nearly 50 percent are minor children (Bureau of Public Affairs, 2004, p. 1; Human Smuggling and Trafficking Center, 2006, p. 1; Miller, Decker, Silverman, & Raj, 2007, p. 486; Shigekane, 2007, p. 113; United States Department of Health and Human Services, n.d.). Considered to be modern slavery, human trafficking involves through force or the threat of force, coercion, deception, and manipulation. Victims may become domestic servants or general laborers, but trafficking for sex is one of the more lucrative businesses. Sex trafficking involves not only international persons, but individuals already residing in the United States being trafficked from state to state. When trafficked individuals become involved within the criminal justice system, they are often identified as prostitutes and are subject to arrest and prosecution, while individuals and organizations who forced them into such positions continue to operate (Human Smuggling and Trafficking Center, 2006, p. 1, 4; Melby, 2004).

Human trafficking can sometimes be mistaken for smuggling, as the differences between victim and perpetrator become blurred. To put the definition of "trafficking" into perspective, "smuggling," although similar to trafficking, has several important differences:

- The individual being smuggled is most often cooperating with the smuggler in order to achieve entry into another country illegally.
- Trafficking can occur within a community, but smuggling always

involves the crossing of an international border.

- Once they arrive in a new country, individuals who have been smuggled are generally free to leave and go about their lives without additional threat of servitude or enslavement.

- Most importantly, individuals who are smuggled are considered to be complicit in the completion of a crime. Although some exceptions to this generalization do exist, smuggled individuals are not considered to be "victims" and are culpable for their crime (Human Smuggling and Trafficking Center, 2006, p. 4).

Potential problems could arise as individuals who may not fall into the criteria of being "trafficked" are, in turn, prosecuted.

Sex trafficking is the most common form of human trafficking, with hundreds of thousands of women and children being used as prostitutes and sexual slaves each year. Some of these women are kidnapped and sold into trafficking, and others are lured under the pretence of marriage or domestic employment. Once trafficked, victims are unable to leave due to the violence, or threat of violence, perpetrated by their captors. Traffickers may also withhold the victims' identification papers or passports, and feed into victims' fears about contacting the police and immigration officials. Victims are constantly being moved by traffickers, ensuring that relationships are not formed with others (Miller et al., 2007, p. 488).

The position taken here is that individuals who are trafficked, forced into prostitution, or both, need assistance from the courts in terms of victim's services, and should not be prosecuted for crimes committed against their will. Although the United States Federal Government has made provisions to assist victims of trafficking, prostitution is often overlooked because of the presiding belief that it is a "victimless crime" (Conyers, 2007; Melby, 2004). However, many victims of trafficking and prostitution develop adverse psychological disorders, including Post-Traumatic Stress Disorder (PTSD), and anxiety disorders due to emotional, physical, and sexual abuse that accompanies sexual servitude. Unfortunately, trafficking victims are sometimes only identified after being arrested for prostitution. Although studies indicate that most women do not want to be involved in prostitution or sexual slavery, discerning a trafficking victim from a "traditional prostitute" becomes difficult, for victims are reluctant to testify against their captors, feeding a continuous cycle of subsequent arrests.

The Link between Prostitution and Sex Trafficking

One of the barriers to identifying prostitutes as victims of trafficking is the societal view of prostitution and related occupations. Research often focuses on health risks, taking the view that prostitution is a choice, which perpetuates the belief that prostitution is a victimless crime, with no visible harm to any one person. However, research indicates that most individuals involved in prostitution do want to leave, but may not be able to for reasons ranging from lack of other skills or available jobs to physical force (Farley, 2004b; Farley et al., 2003, p. 48).

Prostitution is also considered by some to be an occupation, that men purchasing sex is "normal," and inherently engrained in our culture. Distain for the job is viewed no differently than distain for any other unpleasant working environment. Some organizations and focus groups go as far as to call for decriminalization of prostitution and unionization of sex workers, arguing that legitimizing prostitution as a service removes stigma and other adverse effects. Reality indicates that decriminalizing prostitution only alleviates the criminal activities of consumers and pimps. When viewing prostitution in terms of its effects of its victims, as one researcher explains: " [...] unionizing prostituted women makes as little sense as unionizing battered women" (Farley, 2004a, pp. 1089, 1108; Raymond, 2003).

Research conducted by the United States Government indicates that prostitution drives sex trafficking, and as long as a market for sexual labor exists, trafficking will continue to happen in order to provide workers for this market. When prostitution is tolerated, or even decriminalized, the demand for commercialized sex increases, causing more victims to be trafficked to certain areas. "Johns" can conduct illegal operations more freely, operating below the radar of authorities. When communities develop programs for licensure or medical treatment, again, sex trafficking increases, canceling the efforts of such programs. Overall, such programs are not focusing on the core of the issue: the physical, sexual, and psychological victimization of thousands (Bureau of Public Affairs, 2004; Raymond, 2003).

In 2002, Germany fully decriminalized prostitution, after years of gradual acceptance since 1993. Immediately, officials became aware that nearly 75 percent of the sex workers operating in Germany were foreign-born. Estimates now put that number at nearly 85 percent (Raymond, 2003). Since most of the foreign-born sex workers are of a lower economic class, it is nearly impossible to entertain the notion that these women funded their own traveling, leading to the most viable explanation being trafficking (Raymond, 2003). Other countries have reported as well an increase in sex trafficking since decriminalization of prostitution. According to one researcher, trafficking is prostitution, and difficulties arise when trying to distinguish one from the other (Farley, 2004b).

Evidence of Psychological Trauma

Most studies that involve prostitution focus on the adverse physical outcomes, such as sexually transmitted diseases and other ailments, substance dependence and abuse, physical abuse, and sexual abuse. Within the last several years, however, researchers have begun to investigate the adverse psychological effects of prostitution, as more and more evidence surfaces that prostitutes are presenting symptoms of severe psychological disorders, including PTSD and dissociative disorders. Some researchers have suggested that prostitutes, regardless of whether they have been trafficked, show similar mental health outcomes as victims of domestic violence or survivors of sexual assault. Nearly all of the research and documentation reviewed indicates the inherent lack of research into this particular subject area and calls for greater review of prostitute mental health.

In a study conducted by Valera, Sawyer, and Schiraldi in 2000, a sample of 100 prostitutes in inner-city Washington D.C. completed the PTSD Checklist (PCL). The sample was composed of male, female, and transgender male prostitutes who were considered "street" prostitutes, meaning that the primary location of their prostitution took place on city streets. Overall, participants in the study met the criteria for PTSD 42 percent of the time, with men showing significantly higher levels than transgender men in the sample. Apart from meeting the diagnostic criteria for PTSD, as described in the Diagnostic and Statistical Manual of Mental Disorders (DSM-IV-TR), study participants, mostly women, reported severe incidents of physical and sexual assault (pp. 149-53).

In an effort to minimize the effects of prostitution, the country of New Zealand decriminalized prostitution in 2003 by a one vote majority in Parliament. Researcher and clinical psychologist Melissa Farley, who has practiced for over 35 years and authored numerous publications regarding prostitution and trafficking, examines the aftermath of the prostitution law change, along with other available literature relating to the subject, in a 2004 article (Farley, 2004a, p. 1087). According to Farley, regardless of the legal status, prostitution is still harmful to women, for many of the adverse effects have more to do with circumstance rather than actual physical harm. Women involved in prostitution report that verbal abuse is just as damaging, if not more, as physical abuse; and many women report acute and chronic psychological conditions while engaging in prostitution (Farley, 2004a, pp. 1103-4).

Other studies have found that women who are compelled into prostitution, due to the accompanying psychological and social manipulation, have similar levels of PTSD and depression as women who had been raped as a result of force or threat of force (Farley, 2004a, p. 1104). Along with major mental disorders, women in prostitution report relationship difficulties with chosen intimate partners, and feelings of disassociation and dysfunction during sexual intercourse. Disassociation is commonly reported among street-, escort-, and strip-club-prostitutes as a way to emotionally distance themselves from paid sexual encounters.

Research has also demonstrated similar feelings of dissociation among children who are victims of sexual assault, battered women, and tortured prisoners of war (Farley, 2004a, pp. 1105-6). Dissociation, as described by some prostitutes, is necessary for survival (Farley, 2004a, p. 1106). Such psychological mechanisms allow prostitutes to cope with their situations.

In 2003, Farley, along with a team of colleagues, conducted a massive research study of former and current prostitutes from nine different countries. Eight-hundred-and-fifty-four participants, representing Canada, Colombia, Germany, Mexico, South Africa, Thailand, Turkey, the United States, and Zambia, were asked to complete the Prostitution Questionnaire (PQ), the PCL, and the Chronic Health Problems Questionnaire (CHPQ) as part of the study. All questionnaires were available in different languages, and were sometimes read aloud to participants. Subjects were found in a variety of different locales and areas, ranging from street prostitutes to escorts. Some had been trafficked to the areas in which they now prostituted; others were in or near their municipality of origin (Farley et al., 2003, pp. 33-4, 37-42). Overall, 68 percent of participants met the criteria for PTSD. The highest percentage who met the criteria, 86 percent, were from Colombia, and the lowest percentage, 54 percent, were from Mexico (Farley et al., 2003, pp. 44,7). The results indicate that, across all sub-groups, the majority of prostitutes in the sample experienced symptoms of traumatic stress disorder.

Although no specific questionnaire was given, 17 percent of study participants described symptoms of other psychological disorders, including depressive thoughts and suicidal ideations, flashbacks from previous abuse situations, anxiety, tension, and mood swings (Farley et al., 2003, p. 53). This finding parallels findings from other research studies. A 2001 study by Raymond & Hughes found that over 80 percent of domestically and internationally trafficked women experienced depression. Ross, Farley, & Schwartz (2003) found that anxiety and dissociative disorders are common among prostitutes.

Participants in the Farley and colleagues (2003) study also reported a wide variety of neurological and physical ailments, such as gastrointestinal problems, dizziness, numbness, seizures, memory loss, and joint pain (p. 53). Eighty percent reported experiencing verbal abuse and social contempt; the researchers again reiterated the need for further research in this area. The researchers also reported that a long-term consequence of prostitution is Complex PTSD (CPTSD), a condition that results from continued traumatic stress, from captivity, and from complete control by another. Such a disorder may cause an individual to assume the identity that the captor demands, and such an identity is resistant to change (Farley et al., 2003, p. 58).

The effects of prostitution continue even after an individual is no longer involved. Thirty-eight percent of physical problems that were reported in the Farley and colleagues (2003) study were reported more frequently by former prostitutes than current prostitutes (p. 59). Psychological issues have also been found to linger. According to a 2001 study comparing current Canadian prostitutes to former prostitutes, former prostitutes had slightly lower rates of depression but higher rates of anxiety and emotional trauma (Benoit & Millar, 2001).

University of Leeds researcher Teela Sanders completed an interesting study in 2004 that examined prostitutes' perceptions of risk in a large, British city over a 10-month period. Instead of focusing on street prostitutes, Sanders' participant selection was largely indoor workers who all claimed to have entered prostitution voluntarily (Sanders, 2004, pp. 557-8, 61). Arguably, they were at a lesser risk of physical harm than street prostitutes, so it is not surprising that they found the emotional consequences of prostitution more significant than the physical consequences (Sanders, 2004, pp. 566, 70). However, participants still indicated adverse psychological outcomes, most notably being the inability to maintain effective intimate relationships. Prostitutes in this study indicated that they went to great lengths to maintain a dichotomy between sex and making love. This was, often times, accomplished through physical means, such as denying certain sex acts or body parts to customers in order to "save" them for intimate relationships. Some prostitutes refrained from personal, intimate relationships completely while prostituting (Sanders, 2004, p. 567).

One of the main areas of psychological distress in this study related to participants' fears of discovery by friends and family. Worry was constant at "work" and at home, never allowing room for a "mental break." Even though many made great efforts to prevent accidental encounters, to the point of overlooking possible physical risks, the fear of losing family and friends due to their involvement with prostitution continued to persist (Sanders, 2004, pp. 568, 570). This study shows that, even apart from trafficking, psychological manipulations, and abuse, psychological risks still occur in prostitution. Compounded by traumatic experience and threat of violence, the psychological distress experienced by sex workers becomes immense.

Conclusion

Overall, available research confirms that adverse psychological consequences do exist for prostitutes. Those risks are compounded when an individual is forced into prostitution through trafficking, is a victim of sexual and physical abuse, is subject to manipulation, or is held in captivity, either by force or threat of force. Research indicates that such prolonged treatment leaves victims at risk for developing traumatic stress disorders, such as PTSD, at the same levels as battered women and tortured prisoners of war (Farley et al., 2003; Farley, 2004a; Farley, 2004b; Raymond, 2003). The issues are often overlooked in the research, possibly fueled by society's view of prostitution as a "victimless crime" (Farley, 2004b; Farley et al., 2003). Such a view assumes that women who are prostitutes are doing so by their own free will, and overlooks the women who had been forced into prostitution through trafficking.

Trafficking victims are, often times, discovered through arrest for prostitution. Even after victims' circumstances are revealed, they need to prove coercion and cooperate with the authorities in order to evade prosecution. Most women, however, are fearful of the police and not likely to assist investigators, subjecting themselves to numerous arrests and jail stays. Victims who do decide to assist with the investigation, testify, or both, are still subject to significant lengths of incarceration while trials are carried out (Bolger, 2007; Conyers, 2007; Melby, 2004). Although, while victims of other violent crimes may be arrested subsequent to investigation, for the most part, they are not subject to incarceration during the course of the investigation or during criminal proceedings. The only difference between trafficking victims who are forced to prostitute and other victims is the exchange of money; psychological, and even physical effects, are similar. Trafficking and forced-prostitution victims need the assistance of the criminal justice system. They do not need to be treated like criminals.

Questions for Discussion

1. Should the United States grant victims of sex trafficking citizenship? What are the legal ramifications of granting citizenship?
2. What can the justice system do to help victims of sex trafficking?
3. How can the distinction between those who are victims of human trafficking and those engaged in prostitution be clarified to the public?
4. How effective are criminal justice professionals at identifying victims of human trafficking compared with those who are simply engaged in prostitution?

References

Benoit, C., & Millar, A. (2001). *Dispelling myths and understanding realities: Working conditions, health status, and exiting experiences of sex workers.* Retrieved from http://www.understandingsexwork.com/

Bolger, T. (2007, June 22). Slave: Human trafficking on Long Island. Long Island Press. Retrieved July 25, 2007 from

http://www.longislandpress.com/main.asp?SectionID=
2&SubSectionID=2&ArticleID=12434&TM=39663.04

Bureau of Public Affairs (2004, November). *The link between prostitution and sex trafficking*. Retrieved from United States Department of State website: http://www. state.gov

Conyers, J. (2007). The 2005 reauthorization of the Violence Against Women Act: Why Congress acted to expand protections to immigrant victims. *Violence Against Women, 13*(5), 457-468.

Farley, M. (2004a). "Bad for the body, bad for the heart": Prostitution harms women even is legalized or decriminalized. *Violence Against Women, 10*(10), 1087-1125.

Farley, M. (2004b). Prostitution is sexual violence [Special Issue]. *Psychiatric Times*, p. S7.

Farley, M., Cotton, A., Lynne, J., Zumbeck, S., Spiwak, F., Reyes, M.E., Alvarez, D., & Sezgin, U. (2003). Prostitution and trafficking in nine countries: An update on violence and Post-Traumatic Stress Disorder. *Journal of Trauma Practice, 2*(3/4), 33-74.

Human Trafficking and Smuggling Center (2007, April). *Fact sheet: Distinctions between human smuggling and human trafficking*. Retrieved from United States Department of State website: http://www.state.gov/

Melby, T. (2004). Spotlight on a hidden crime: U.S. targets sexual slavery worldwide and within its own borders. *Contemporary Sexuality, 38*(5), 1-6.

Miller, E., Decker, M.R., Silverman, J.G., & Raj, A. (2007). Migration, sexual exploitation, and women's health: A case report from a community health center. *Violence Against Women, 13*(5), 486-497.

Raymond, J.G. (2003). 10 reasons for not legalizing prostitution. Retrieved July 25, 2007 from Prostitution Research and Education Web site: http://www.prostitutionresearch.com/laws 000022.html.

Raymond, J.G., & Hughes, D.M. (2001). *Sex trafficking of women in the United States: International and domestic trends*. Retrieved from U.S. Department of Justice, Office of Justice Programs, National Criminal Justice Reference Service website: https://www.ncjrs.gov/

Ross, C.A., Farley, M., & Schwartz, H.L. (2003). Dissociation Among Women in Prostitution. In M. Farley (Ed.), *Prostitution, trafficking, and traumatic stress*. Binghamton, NY: The Haworth Press, Inc.

Sanders, T. (2004). A continuum of risk? The management of health, physical and emotional risks by female sex workers. *Sociology of Health and Illness, 26*(5), 557-574.

Shigekane, R. (2007). Rehabilitation and community integration of trafficking survivors in the United States. *Human Rights Quarterly, 29*(1), 112-126.

United States Department of Health and Human Services, Administration for Children and Families (n.d.). *About human trafficking: Overview of human trafficking issue.* Retrieved July 24, 2007, from http://www.acf.hhs.gov/trafficking/about/index.html.

Valera, R.J., Sawyer, R.G., & Schiraldi, G.R. (2000). Violence and Post-Traumatic Stress Disorder in a campus on inner city street prostitutes. *American Journal of Health Studies, 16*(3), 149-155

6 POLICE STRESS AND TRAUMATIC STRESS

Stress is a commonality in every aspect of life. Stress in law enforcement is a result of a traumatic event experienced and the response to the event by an officer. The most simplistic way to express the relationship between the individual and the traumatic event is by presenting the potential for the disorder from the individual's perspective. This relationship is also closely related to the General Adaptation Syndrome (GAS) diathesis-stress model developed by Hans Selye (1973). According to Barlow and Durand (2005), the main point of the model is that the individual may either have a generalized psychological vulnerability, or have a generalized biological vulnerability to stress.

Norvell, Hills and Murrin (1993) were interested in the perception of stress levels as influenced by physical symptoms and job dissatisfaction. A higher number of physical symptoms and job dissatisfaction contribute to the perception of increased stress in law enforcement male and female officers (Norvell et al., 1993). Also, when female officers were assessed separately, female officers experienced a significantly smaller level of distress and dissatisfaction compared to male counterparts (Norvell et al., 1993).

Defining stress

Stress is defined by considering three types of life events:
- Explosive incidents
- Implosive incidents
- Corrosive incidents (Waters & Ussery, 2007).

Explosive incidents are those that are major disasters, natural or man-made, and crimes that are in progress (Waters & Ussery, 2007). Implosive incidents are those that can arise out of a disparity between thoughts and behaviors, such as an internal conflict about an officer's effectiveness (Waters & Ussery, 2007). Finally, corrosive incidents are those that eat away at an officer a little bit at a time, and are small annoyances that build up on a daily basis (Waters & Ussery, 2007).

Stress is also referred to as an inner state of strain or disturbance that is externally characterized by anxiety or frustration (Haarr & Morash, 1999). These disturbances can manifest in an officer just as easily as in anyone else. "The day-to-day stress of dealing with people and their problems, especially the deeply disturbing aspects of dealing with critical incidents, can traumatize officers and poison their spirits" (Harpold & Feemster, 2002). Some have called this day-to-day stress progressive job stress (Metcalf, 1985). In addition to the progressive job stress, Metcalf (1985) identified a departmental stress creator. This departmental stress, according to Metcalf (1985), arises when a department dictates less important aspects of the job, such as cutting hair a certain length or shining shoes appropriately, and leaves critical aspects undefined, such as when to use deadly force.

Current state of stress and law enforcement

Occupational stress is no stranger to law enforcement officers. Studies have been conducted that assess the correlation between occupational stress and job performance. One such study by Liberman, Best, Metzler, Fagan, Weiss, and Marmar (2002) considered the occupational stress experienced by law enforcement officers as compared with the level of psychological distress experienced. The study assessed two areas of routine occupational stress. First, the researchers found that being habitually exposed to occupational stress can directly predict the psychological distress that urban police officers will experience (Liberman et al., 2002). Second, Liberman and colleagues (2002) found that urban police officers who experience habitual occupational stress were more susceptible to psychological distress than those exposed to an accumulation of critical incidents or traumatic events. Regardless of the task in law enforcement, one is sure to struggle with psychological trauma.

Habitual occupational stress has been examined in connection with policing tasks of varying degrees of difficulty. A study conducted by Brown, Fielding and Grover (1999) considered less predictable features in an officer's work environment. Brown and colleagues (1999) found traffic officers to be "more susceptible to stress than other uniformed colleagues or detectives" (p. 323). This finding was indicative of the unforeseeable outcome in a traffic stop. The officers could not know beforehand whether the traffic stop would go smoothly or would become violent and threatening to the officer's life, causing elevated levels of stress.

Occupational stress has been researched between male and female officers (McCarty, Zhao & Garland, 2007). Data was collected with respect to occupational stress and burnout between male and female police officers. In this study, ethnicity was not a predictor of occupational stress or burnout. The researchers also found that there was little difference between male and female occupational stress and burnout. However, coping mechanisms and perception of unfairness were two factors considered to be predictors of occupational stress in both male and female officers.

The frequency of traumatic events in the life of a law enforcement officer is critical. Law enforcement officers enter that career with the understanding that traumatic situations are likely to occur at least once during each shift. Despite the understanding that dangerous situations will be encountered, officers are not immune to the effects of stressors (Renck, Weisæth & Skarbö, 2002). Since this is understood in the field of law enforcement, the frequency of traumatic events is important in determining how much impact it will have on the officer.

A plethora of events can contribute to increased stress levels in law enforcement officers and administrators. Several factors have been described as contributing to the increase of stress experienced by law enforcement supervisors, such as:

- A disparity between compensation and responsibility.
- Being asked to act as a motivator and disciplinarian.
- A lack of concretely defined job descriptions and expectations (Trojanowicz, 1980).

Unmarried and inexperienced police officers tend to be at higher risk for increased stress (Kirkcaldy, Brown & Cooper, 1998).

Superintendents of police organizations experience stress because of internal factors such as "inadequate guidance and support from superiors, insufficient consultation and communication, inadequate feedback, lack of adequate finances or resources, and staff shortages and disturbing turnover rates" (Brown, Cooper & Kirkcaldy, 1996, p. 36). Though the levels of stress in officers from larger police agencies is not significantly different than those of smaller police agencies, officers from larger agencies report slightly more stress (Brooks & Piquero, 1998). Brown and colleagues (1999) found that high-impact stressors experienced with low frequency were associated with an increased likelihood of experiencing Post-Traumatic Stress Disorder (PTSD) symptoms.

Frustrations specific to campus police chiefs are addressing problematic employees, dealing with upper administration, and facing budget issues – they represent the most discouraging and dissatisfying portions of the job (Benson et al., 2006). Factors reported as having a negative impact on social responsibilities were

- intense stress,

- the constant obligation to the job,
- the amount of time required to perform the duties, and
- physical differences, such as an increase in weight, smoking or drinking, and a decrease in physical fitness (Benson et al., 2006).

Moving from Stress to Post-Traumatic Stress Disorder

Law enforcement is no stranger to stressful and traumatic situations that strain one's mental stamina. Daily, officers enter their departments with the understanding that they are willingly placing themselves in potentially traumatic settings. When one of these traumatic events occurs, the law enforcement officer must have a strategic plan of action in place to guard against PTSD. Within the field of law enforcement, PTSD has a history that serves to illustrate the severity of the traumatic event of the day, the level of resiliency of affected individuals, and the efficacy of various interventions.

The most primitive descriptions of PTSD in the United States can be traced to the military feuds of the mid-19th century. The prevailing assumption of these descriptions was that PTSD had biological causes. Since the third edition of the Diagnostic and Statistical Manual of Mental Disorders (American Psychiatric Association [APA], 1980; American Psychiatric Association [APA], 2000; American Psychiatric Association [APA], 2013), a clinical description outlining all of the symptoms has been available. Despite the more recent notions that the disorder is wholly psychological, there are indications that PTSD has biological causes such as lesions on brain structures or neurotransmitter deficiencies.

When considering the effects of police stress, the nature of the individual involved must be considered. The predisposition to acquire a disorder is important to establishing an appropriate prognosis. Similarly, the nature of the traumatic event must not be overlooked. The frequency and intensity of the trauma plays a part in the prognosis of the disorder. The initial stages are considered to be the warning signs, which can flag a department manager to the possibility of losing an officer to the debilitating effects of PTSD. In law enforcement, these initial stages can come in the form of

- witnessing a fellow officer commit suicide,
- shooting an innocent person, or
- being on the scene of a major traumatic event.

The events of September 11th and Hurricane Katrina are two examples of recent major traumatic events that have affected law enforcement. Discoveries regarding the severity of PTSD have led to refinement of psychological and psychopharmacological interventions.

A Brief History and Overview of PTSD

For approximately the last 135 years, symptoms of PTSD have been documented in the United States. In America during the mid-19th century, PTSD was referred to as "irritable heart" and "soldiers' heart" (Lamprecht & Sack, 2002, p. 222; Ray, 2006, p. 1; van der Kolk, McFarlane & Weisaeth, 1996, p.48). Since the publication of the Diagnostic and Statistical Manual of Mental Disorders, Third Edition [DSM-III] (APA, 1980), this set of symptoms has been given the formal name of Post-Traumatic Stress Disorder (PTSD). With regard to PTSD, most of the research conducted has been done on those with military experience.

Shortly after the Civil War in America there began an epidemic among those who were in the midst of conflict. In 1870 and 1871, two men considered the symptoms of what they called irritable heart and soldiers' heart. These two men, Arthur Bowen Richards Myers and Jacob Da Costa, combined their efforts with regard to post-war psychological adaptation. A. B. R. Myers was the first of the two to describe the disorder, and both men found this problem "so frequently in soldiers with fighting experience that they gave it a diagnostic term of its own: 'irritable heart' or 'soldier's heart'" (Lamprecht & Sack, 2002, p. 222).

Lewis (1940) lists and describes several characteristics of this early diagnosis of what was thought to be a physiological disease, including symptoms of breathlessness due to a constriction of muscles. Additional symptoms outlined were fatigue and exhaustion, accompanied by tension related to tightened chest muscles. Fainting, headaches, increased heart rate, and increased blood pressure were also listed as common symptoms for those who were diagnosed with the soldier's heart (pp. 26-39). Lewis and some other men studied the causes and symptoms of the condition, and were convinced that it was simply due to biological causes.

Many of the early researchers who studied PTSD symptoms had sought to define the symptoms based on the situation to which the condition was attributed. A man named John Eric Erichsen, while in England, described it as damage to the spinal cord. He named this condition "Railway Spine Syndrome" (Levy, 1995, p. 2; Miller, 1997, p. 21; Ray, 2006, p. 2). He coined this term because the symptoms were similar to those of Da Costa and Myers, but the situation was not war, but rather the expansion of the railroad system in the middle to late 1800's. Some have considered the describing of Railway Spine Syndrome the "beginning of the scientific description of traumatic neuroses" (Miller, 1997, p. 21).

Much controversy arose out of the description given by Charles Samuel Myers, who was a military psychiatrist. He ideated and concluded that post-war shock was a direct result of tiny sections of exploded bombs entering the brain. He termed this disease "Shell Shock," and was the first to use the term in medical publications (Ray, 2006, p. 2; van der Kolk et al., 1996, p.

48). Gradually, the belief that this condition was purely medical faded away due to cases found in those who had no exposure to gunfire. These findings gave way to the assumption that the causes of these symptoms were completely emotional. This misconception about the causes of Shell Shock played an important role in eliminating the presupposition that there was a correlation between traumatic stress and biological factors.

The major event that changed the course of how psychiatrists and psychologists have looked at traumatic stress was the Vietnam War. Prior to the Vietnam War, the DSM-I (American Psychiatric Association [APA], 1952) introduced a term to deal with the increasing prevalence of the condition. In the first edition of the DSM, the words "gross stress reaction" (Lamprecht & Sack, 2002, p. 225) were used to explain the set of symptoms that is currently called PTSD. This term was quickly replaced by the term found in the DSM-II (American Psychiatric Association [APA], 1968) "transient situation disturbance" (Lamprecht & Sack, 2002, p. 225). Transient situation disturbance included such things as psychotic reactions as a consequence of devastating stress. Both of these editions of the DSM lacked any form of operational definition by which clinicians could adequately diagnose the disorder in patients. The first time that PTSD appeared in an edition of the DSM was in 1980, when it was published in the DSM-III. The Vietnam War is the main reason that the American Psychological Association has placed PTSD in their Diagnostic and Statistical Manual of Mental Disorders. The veterans of the war insisted that it be a recognized disorder (Levy, 1995, p. 2; National Vietnam Veterans Art Museum, n.d., p. 4). This was the first time that this type of disorder had clear criteria laid out in a diagnostic manual. This gave clinicians specific descriptions to adhere to in their diagnoses. Since its first appearance in the DSM-III, PTSD has been clarified and enhanced to create more consistency between clinicians.

Officers with PTSD are, often times, placed in everyday situations that exacerbate their levels of stress. Sheehan and Van Hasselt (2003) indicate that these on-the-job stressors can range from participating in specialized duties by an officer –examples include

- being placed in an undercover situation,
- taking part in a crisis or hostage negotiation, or
- not having the ability to control life's situations. (p. 13)

These are stressors related to police work, but there are also family stressors that can trigger symptoms of PTSD. These could include an unstable marriage or a death in the family. It is also important to note that "natural changes to all of the body's systems have strong consequences" (Sheehan & Van Hasselt, 2003, p. 13). These changes include such things as going through the body's natural aging, being in an unfulfilling relationship, or lacking in spiritual meaning.

The Nature of the Individual and the Traumatic Event

The symptoms of PTSD are not only a result of the traumatic event that was experienced, but also a result of the person who experienced the traumatic event. Both aspects must be considered when making an adequate assessment of the diagnoses related to PTSD. The simplest way to express the relationship between the individual and the traumatic event is by presenting the potential for the disorder from the individual's perspective. This is also closely related to the GAS diathesis-stress model developed by Hans Selye (Selye, 1973). According to Barlow & Durand (2005), the main point of the model is that the individual either may have a generalized psychological vulnerability or may have a generalized biological vulnerability to traumatic stress.

The individual who has one of these and who comes into contact with a stressful or traumatic life event will most likely develop PTSD. This model is not fool-proof; rather it is merely a generality that helps indicate the potential problems that may arise (p. 158). This model helps clinicians determine the likelihood of an individual to develop the PTSD symptoms.

Just because a person is likely to develop symptoms of PTSD does not mean that the person will develop those symptoms. There are two categories of factors that affect the likelihood of individuals developing PTSD symptoms. Alloy, Riskind & Manos (2005) considered the features of the trauma experienced and the features of the person who experienced that trauma (p. 160).

The features of the traumatic event are as follows:

- The intensity of the trauma.
- The duration to which the person was exposed to the trauma.
- The extent of the threat of the trauma.
- The nature of the trauma (Alloy et al., 2005, p. 160).

The first feature, the intensity of the traumatic event, is the amount of the trauma that is experienced by the individual. In the case of the September 11th terrorist attacks, this would be the difference between being five blocks from ground zero and being five miles from ground zero. The second is the duration to which the individual is exposed to the trauma. In the case of a Vietnam veteran, it would be the difference between spending three months in combat or six months in combat. The third is the extent to which the traumatic event is life threatening. In the case of a rape victim, this would mean the difference between the deviant having a weapon as opposed to having no weapon. Lastly, the nature of the event must be taken into account. This point takes into consideration that the trauma can have differing effects if it is created by humans, such as the events of September 11th, or if humans have no control over it, such as Hurricane Katrina. These four features consider the effects of an actual event on the person, but do not address the vulnerabilities of the person.

The features of the person, as stated by Alloy and colleagues (2005), are

- pretraumatic psychological adaptability,
- family psychopathology,
- cognitive and coping skills, and
- the feelings of guilt. (p. 160)

Pretraumatic psychological adaptability is important because, if the individual is unable to bounce back after a normal, less-stressful event, then it is almost certain that the individual will be unable to recover after a more traumatic event. Secondly, family psychopathology, or a history of psychological disorders in the individual's family, may cause an increased tendency to develop the same disorder. Thirdly, the cognitive and coping skills are important because an individual must be able to effectively cope with stressful or traumatic events. The final feature is the feeling of guilt, where the person feels guilty or responsible for a traumatic event – especially if some other person loses his or her life in the same event – and this will not be able to return to normal functioning as quickly.

Several other features of individuals with PTSD have been researched. Memory with regard to stressful situations has been analyzed (Beehr, Ivanitskaya, Glaser, Erofeev & Canali, 2004) as well as occupational stress in connection with psychological distress (Liberman et al., 2002), and occupational stress in connection with an unpredictable situational outcome (Brown, Fielding & Grover, 1999). The details surrounding the imminent danger were positively correlated, the less threatening the detail, the more negatively they were correlated (Beehr, et al., 2004, p. 228). The hippocampus is directly related to the encoding of memories and to the initiating hormonal response to fear or anxiety; therefore, the correlation between memories and stressful events is apparent.

Occupational stress is no stranger to law enforcement officers. A correlation exists between occupational stress and job performance that has sparked much research. One such study by Liberman and colleagues (2002) considered the level of occupational stress experienced by law enforcement officers as compared with the level of psychological distress experienced. The study of urban police officers assessed two areas of routine occupational stress. First, they found that being habitually exposed to occupational stress can directly predict the psychological distress that the individual will experience. Second, they found that urban police officers who were exposed to habitual occupational stress showed greater potential for acquiring psychological distress than a cumulative exposure to critical incidents or traumatic events (p. 432). Regardless of the task in law enforcement, one is sure to be a companion of psychological trauma.

The Initial Stages of Post-Traumatic Stress Disorder

Stress is a direct result of our appraisal of and coping with life events (Myers, 2005, p. 402). A person, when faced with a situation in life, approaches it expecting to make a decision about that situation. The decision that is made typically involves first assessing it as a threat or as a challenge to the person's being. In either case, the autonomic nervous system is involved. When an individual assesses a situation as a threat, he or she will experience more psychological distress then if he or she were to assess the situation as a challenge. However, even though the individual may experience more psychological distress, this does not necessarily mean that the person will experience enough to cause symptoms of PTSD.

Three categories or levels of stressors can exist in the lifetime of any individual. The three types of stressors, organized by increasing level of stress, are as follows:

- Daily hassles
- Significant life changes
- Catastrophes

In order, each of these stressor types becomes progressively more strenuous on the individual. Daily hassles are just that; they are things that can become annoyances but do not, by themselves, create a significant amount of stress. Daily hassles can be anything from slow moving traffic to a spouse leaving toothpaste in the bathroom sink. Significant life changes are the second level of stressors. Some significant life changes are marriage, divorce, or the loss of a job. These events are things that do not occur daily but carry with them a significant amount of stress. The third stressor type, catastrophes, are unpredictable events that most people in a society view as being threatening, and are the most stress causing. These are large-scale events that affect each person in the society differently. Examples in recent years are the events of September 11, 2001 and Hurricane Katrina, among others. It is this third category of stressors that are most likely to be the origin of the symptoms of PTSD (Myers, 2005, pp. 404-405).

The first level of stressors is of moderate focus in the study of the stages of PTSD symptoms and causation. As concluded by Liberman and colleagues (2002), cited earlier, continuous exposure to daily hassles are actually more stress causing than the compilation of critical incidents. Similarly, positive and negative emotions have much to do with job satisfaction and with mood within employment. Kohan & O'Connor (2002) considered the relevance of life satisfaction and job satisfaction to job stress. They found that positive emotional experiences were directly correlated with both job satisfaction and life satisfaction (p. 314). Those individuals who took part in the survey indicated that they felt better about their job and life when there was reason to feel better, such as relationships interacting well or receiving praise for jobs well done.

One study conducted by Jaramillo, Nixon & Sams (2005) considers the organizational commitments held by those who have been affected by law enforcement stress. Supervisor support, group cohesiveness and promotional opportunities contribute to the commitment to the organization by an individual. Although job satisfaction is the most important contributor to organizational commitment, these three also contribute. When supervisor support is high, group cohesiveness between police officers and management is strong. Further, when promotional opportunities are available, there is a much stronger desire to remain within the department that one is serving.

The second level of stressor is significant life changes. These are similar to the first level in that they can contribute to the positive affect of an individual when situations are positive, but can create disastrous symptoms when situations are not positive. While getting married or having a baby are wonderfully positive events, they carry stressors with them. The act of getting married, with all of the events leading up to that day, can produce significant amounts of fear and apprehension similar to having a baby or to losing a job. These events, if experienced frequently, may mark the beginning of PTSD symptoms. Although the culminating of the life-change events is not likely to be the problem, it could be one major event after a string of significant life-change events that sends an individual "into a tailspin".

In the context of PTSD, those stressors in the third level have been given a name: critical incidents. It is the critical incidents that are so widely researched in connection with PTSD patients. Kureczka (1996) defines a critical incident as "any event that has a stressful impact sufficient to overwhelm the usually effective coping skills of an individual" (p. 10). Within society, as mentioned already, two critical-incident examples are September 11, 2001 and Hurricane Katrina. For a law enforcement officer, these critical incidents can be the death of a fellow officer while on duty, severe injury to a fellow officer while on duty, or an officer suicide. Kureczka (1996) also points out wisely that the definition of critical incidents must "remain fluid" in order to encompass all types of stressors (p. 10). The reason for this is simply because not all stressors affect each person the same way. Kureczka (1996) continues to elaborate on the stress caused by critical incidents when he discusses how the critical incident materializes itself within the individual "physically, cognitively, and emotionally" (p. 11).

The essential task, now, is to determine the "earliest stage possible, when particular law enforcement officers incur an excessive stress reaction to the numerous pressures confronting them" (Sheehan & Van Hasselt, 2003, p. 16).

PTSD in Law Enforcement

The prevalence of stressful situations within law enforcement departments and with corresponding duties has been the focus of many studies connected with PTSD. Inside every department, there are stressors from the plethora of task-related paperwork to critical incidents, such as homicide. Many law enforcement officer stressors can be dealt with in more than one way. Potential stress-relieving methods can include nondetrimental means, such as religion or exercise, or by more detrimental means, such as alcohol or drug abuse (Benson et al., 2006). Law enforcement officers typically experience recurring symptoms of PTSD, such as intrusive thoughts or feelings of isolation, after the stressful situation due to the trauma itself or due to the public and repeated exposure to the stressful situation via departmental reports and court hearings (Mann & Neece, 1990, p. 449)

Law enforcement officers enter their careers with the understanding that they are likely to encounter traumatic situations during their shifts. Despite their understanding that they will encounter dangerous situations in their line of work, they are not immune to the effects of stressors (Renck, Weisæth & Skarbö, 2002, p. 13). Since this is understood in the field of law enforcement, the frequency of a given traumatic event is important for determining how much impact it will have on the officer. Brown and colleagues (1999) studied the effects of stressors of low frequency versus those of high frequency. They found that high-impact stressors experienced with low frequency were associated with the potential of experiencing PTSD symptoms (p. 322).

An example of a high-impact traumatic situation that occurs with low frequency is the 1992 "Los Angeles Riot" (Harvey-Lintz & Tidwell, 1997). At the end of April 1992, civil disturbances broke out; the law enforcement department was seen as an instigator as well as the group expected to bring peace. The officers were not instigators in the sense that they participated in the unrest, but rather that they had little to no support or direction from their management. Additionally, they became overwhelmed and outnumbered by the crowds. Unfavorable conditions on the Los Angeles Police Department (LAPD) included the following:

- The traumatic event of the Los Angeles Riot.
- The fact that residents held the LAPD responsible for the unrest.
- That, prior to this event, tension between the officers and the community existed already (Harvey-Lintz & Tidwell, 1997).

The inability of the officers to maintain the situation caused significant psychological distress for the officers. Far-reaching effects to the officers have been examined in connection with the Los Angeles Riot. These effects have had an impact on almost every area of the officers' lives, including the officers' families, department, community, and society.

Unfortunately, officers with PTSD, who do not have adequate coping skills or social support, often resort to suicide. Similar to PTSD, suicide has been correlated with decreased levels of serotonin in the body. Significant characteristics of those who are suicidal include hopelessness, helplessness, bitterness, and selfishness. Sheehan & Van Hasselt (2003) state, "Sadly, among law enforcement officers, job-related stress frequently contributes to the ultimate maladaptive response to stress: suicide" (p. 16).

Though many officers commit suicide, there has been research that illustrates that law enforcement suicides are not on the rise. A critical review of suicide specifically in police officers, conducted by Hem, Berg & Ekeberg (2001), has found that suicide among law enforcement officers has not necessarily increased compared to other professions. However, they did present substantial evidence that there could be biases within departments to avoid disclosing such information about their respective departments. First, there could be simply a lack of recorded documentation. Second, there could be a breakdown in the reliability of information presented by relatives of suicide victims after 10 years from the suicide, or access to the relevant information may simply be denied based on the fact that the information is sensitive. Third, a study of records accessed by Marzuk, Nock, Leon, Portera & Tardiff (2002) concluded that, in New York City over a span of 19 years from 1977 to 1996, there was not an increase in the ratio of suicides in law enforcement officers to the number of officers employed in the same time frame.

Several characteristics were found to be present in the records assessed by Marzuk and colleagues (2002). These characteristics included that almost every suicide recorded was carried out by the use of a firearm. This is indicative of the familiarity of law enforcement officers with firearms as well as the ease of access to the firearms. Important characteristics related to law enforcement suicides also included marital problems, the abuse of alcohol, and job suspensions. However, age, race, years of service, and ranks of the officers were not related to a risk of suicide. Another study, conducted by Rouse and colleagues (2015), found a challenge to a strong theoretical assertion that exposure to critical incidents, such as officer involved shootings, were not a primary predictors of police suicides. Frequently and unfortunately, a suicide is the first time many departments become aware of any maladaptive behaviors of a given member with their respective force.

There are numerous programs to prevent PTSD symptoms (Amaranto, Steinberg, Castellano, & Mitchell, 2003; Gersons, Carlier, Lamberts, & van der Kolk, 2000; Tolin & Foa, 1999; Ussery & Waters, 2006) from becoming too great. If a department employs a psychologist to assess the members of the department, there is a tendency for members to believe that psychologist will prevent them from doing what they love – law enforcement.

Conclusion

As seen in the history of PTSD from the mid-19th century to the present, PTSD has biological and psychological components. Predispositions to acquiring a disorder and the nature of a given traumatic event corroborate to predict or trigger the symptoms of PTSD. The events of September 11th 2001 and Hurricane Katrina in 2005 serve as reminders to the sphere of law enforcement that they are not invincible. The traumatic events and the aftermath of September 11th left law enforcement officers dazed and vulnerable to PTSD. In the midst of confusion in New York City after the attacks, law enforcement officers were still expected to perform their duties without reprieve or mediocrity. Similarly, the magnitude of trauma from Hurricane Katrina was unanticipated by the law enforcement departments and subsequently evoked traumatic stress in those who were called to service in those areas. All around the world, cases of PTSD have been researched, some by clinical means and others by empirical means.

Numerous interventions have been tried, used, and sometimes abandoned since the beginning of the diagnosis of PTSD. Psychological treatments, such as cognitive behavioral therapy, have been used and adapted to meet the delicate needs of PTSD victims. Psychopharmacological treatments have also been prevalent within the scope of applicable interventions for PTSD. Medications have been found to decrease the severity and frequency of PTSD symptoms. A combination of these two interventions, along with effective and encouraging social support, is vital to the success of coping effectively with PTSD.

Within the field of law enforcement, PTSD has been studied to illustrate the severity of current traumatic events, as well as to measure the efficacy of various interventions. In the face of terrorism and natural disasters, law enforcement officers must be aware of the potential hazards of PTSD and take the proper precautions to avoid the devastating effects of traumatic events and situations, both while on duty and off duty. Whether an officer takes the danger of his or her position seriously can mean the difference between an effective or meager attempt at coping with PTSD.

Questions for Discussion

1. What are the differences between males and females when it comes to occupational stress in law enforcement officers?
2. What are some of the factors that contribute to officer stress from law enforcement supervisors?

3. What are some of the ways that law enforcement officers can deal with the daily job related stressors?

4. What are some of the signs and stress factors of which police administration should be aware?

References

Alloy, L. B., Riskind, J. H. & Manos, M. J. (2005). Abnormal psychology: Current perspectives (9th ed.). New York: McGraw-Hill.

Amaranto, E., Steinberg, J., Castellano, C. & Mitchell, R. (2003). Police stress interventions. *Brief Treatment and Crisis Intervention, 3*(1), 47-53.

American Psychiatric Association. (1952). Diagnostic and Statistical Manual of Mental Disorders (1st Ed.). Washington, DC: American Psychiatric Association.

American Psychiatric Association. (1968). Diagnostic and Statistical Manual of Mental Disorders (2nd Ed.). Washington, DC: American Psychiatric Association.

American Psychiatric Association. (1980). Diagnostic and Statistical Manual of Mental Disorders (3rd Ed.). Washington, DC: American Psychiatric Association.

American Psychiatric Association. (2000). Diagnostic and Statistical Manual of Mental Disorders (4th Ed., Revised Text). Washington, DC: American Psychiatric Association.

American Psychiatric Association. (2013). Diagnostic and Statistical Manual of Mental Disorders (5th Ed.). Washington, DC: American Psychiatric Association.

Barlow, D. H. & Durand, V. M. (2005). Abnormal psychology: An integrative approach. Thompson Wadsworth: CA.

Beehr, T., Ivanitskaya, L., Glaser, K., Erofeev, D. & Canali, K. (2004). Working in a violent environment: The accuracy of police officers' reports about shooting incidents. *Journal of Occupational and Organizational Psychology, 77*, 217-235.

Benson, B. L., Rittereiser, S., and Hwang, E. G. (2006). Addressing the frustrations of campus police chiefs and directors. *Campus Law Enforcement Journal, 36* (5), 6-10.

Brooks, L. W. and Piquero, N. L. (1998). Police stress: Does department size matter? *Policing, 21* (4), 600-617.

Brown, J., Cooper, C., and Kirkcaldy, B. (1996). Occupational stress among senior police officers. *British Journal of Psychology, 87*, 31-41.

Brown, J., Fielding, J. & Grover, J. (1999). Distinguishing traumatic, vicarious and routine operational stressor exposure and attendant adverse consequences in a sample of police officers. *Work & Stress, 13*(4), 312-325.

Gersons, B. P. R., Carlier, I. V. E., Lamberts, R. D. & van der Kolk, B. A. (2000). Randomized clinical trial of brief eclectic psychotherapy for police officers with Post-Traumatic Stress Disorder. *Journal of Traumatic Stress, 13*(2), 333-347.

Haarr, R. N. and Morash, M. (1999). Gender, race, and strategies of coping with occupational stress in policing. *Justice Quarterly, 16* (2), 303-336.

Harpold, J. A. and Feemster, S. L. (2002). Negative influences of police stress. *FBI Law Enforcement Bulletin, 71*(9), 1-7.

Harvey-Lintz, T. & Tidwell, R. (1997). Effects of the 1992 Los Angeles civil unrest: Post-Traumatic Stress Disorder symptomatology among law enforcement officers. *Social Science Journal, 34*(2).

Hem, E., Berg, A. M. & Ekeberg, O. (2001). Suicide in police - A critical review. *Suicide & Life - Threatening Behavior, 31*(2), 224-233.

Jaramillo, F., Nixon, R. & Sams, D. (2005). The effect of law enforcement stress on organizational commitment. *Policing, 28*(2), 321-336.

Kirkcaldy, B., Brown, J. & Cooper, C. L. (1998). The demographics of occupational stress among police superintendents. *Journal of Managerial Psychology, 13*(1/2), 90.

Kohan, A. & O'Connor, B. (2002). Police officer job satisfaction in relation to mood, well-being, and alcohol consumption. *The Journal of Psychology, 136*(3), 307-318.

Kureczka, A. W. (1996). Critical incident stress in law enforcement. *The FBI Law Enforcement Bulletin, 65*(2/3), 10-16.

Lamprecht, F. & Sack, M. (2002). Post-Traumatic Stress Disorder revisited. *Psychosomatic Medicine, 64*, 222-237.

Levy, M. I. (1995). Stressing the point: When is a post traumatic stress disorder claim legitimate . . . and when is it not. ExpertPages.com's Knowledge Base, Retrieved October 26, 2006, from http://expertpages.com/news/ptsd.htm

Lewis, T. (1940). The soldier's heart and the effort syndrome (2nd ed.). London: Shaw & Sons Ltd.

Liberman, A. M., Best, S. R., Metzler, T. J., Fagan, J. A., Weiss, D. S. & Marmar, C. R. (2002). Routine occupational stress and psychological distress in police. *Policing, 25*(2), 421-439.

Mann, J. P. & Neece, J. (1990). Workers' compensation for law enforcement related Post-Traumatic Stress Disorder. *Behavioral Sciences and the Law, 8*, 447-456.

Marzuk, P. M., Nock, M. K., Leon, A. C., Portera, L. & Tardiff, K. (2002). Suicide among New York City police officers, 1977-1996. *The American Journal of Psychiatry, 159*(12), 2069-2071.

McCarty, W. P., Zhao, J., and Garland, B. E. (2007). Occupational stress and burnout between male and female police officers: Are there any gender differences? *Policing: An International Journal of Police Strategies &*

Management, 30 (4), 672-691.

Metcalf, F. (1985). Stress and the police officer. *Campus Law Enforcement Journal, 15* (2), 24-27.

Miller, T. W. (Ed.). (1997). Clinical disorders and stressful life events. Madison, CT: International Universities Press, Inc.

Myers, D. G. (2005). Exploring psychology (6th ed.). Holland, MI: Worth Publishers.

National Vietnam Veterans Art Museum. (n.d.). Trauma & metamorphosis II [Booklet]. Chicago, IL.

Norvell, N. K., Hills, H. A., and Murrin, M. R. (1993). Understanding stress in female and male law enforcement officers. *Psychology of Women Quarterly, 17*, 289-301.

Ray, M. K. PTSD - History and evolution. Retrieved October 26, 2006, Web site: http://www.twilightbridge.com/psychiatryproper/ailmentguide/ptsd/history.htm

Renck, B., Weisaeth, L. & Skarbö, S. (2002). Stress reactions in police officers after a disaster rescue operation. *Nordic Journal of Psychiatry, 56*(7), 7-14.

Rouse, L. M., Frey, R. A., López, M., Wohlers, H., Xiong, I., Llewellyn, K., Lucci, S. P., & Wester, S. R. (2015). Law enforcement suicide: Discerning etiology through psychology autopsy. *Police Quarterly, 18(1)*, 79-108.

Selye, H. (1973). The evolution of the stress concept. *American Scientist, 61* (6), 692-699.

Sheehan, D. C. & Van Hasselt, V. B. (2003). Identifying law enforcement stress reactions early. *The FBI Law Enforcement Bulletin, 72*(9), 12-17.

Tolin, D. F. & Foa, E. B. (1999). Treatment of a police officer with PTSD using prolonged exposure. *Behavior Therapy, 29*(Summer/Fall), 527-538.

Trojanowicz, R. C. (1980). The environment of the first-line police supervisor. Englewood Cliffs, NJ: Prentice-Hall.

Ussery, W. J. & Waters, J. A. (2006). COP-2-COP hotlines: Programs to address the needs of first responders and their families. *Brief Treatment and Crisis Intervention, 6*(1), 66-78.

van der Kolk, B. A., McFarlane, A. C. & Weisaeth, L. (Eds.). (1996). Traumatic stress: The effects of overwhelming experience on mind, body, and society. New York: The Guilford Press.

Waters, J. A. and Ussery, W. (2007). Police stress: History, contributing factors, symptoms, and interventions. *Policing: An International Journal of Police Strategies and Management, 30* (2), 169-188.

7 PRISON REFORM POLICY AND MENTAL HEALTH

Punishment has always been a staple in the United States. Formal punishments in the form of incarceration began with facilities on the East Coast in Pennsylvania and New York. These facilities were not perfect, but had fulfilled the basic requirements to be called penal institutions. Since the dawn of penal institutions in the United States, there have been efforts to reform these facilities. Many of the early reforms focused on structural advances and changes. Today, most of the structural aspects have been solidified into best practices for penal institutions, However, penal policy, including release of inmates, has lagged behind structural advances.

As a frontrunner in almost any policy issue, California has been working hard in recent years to address the gaps in prison reform. California has seen enormous growth in its prison population, which started to become a major governmental issue between 2006 and 2008 (California Department of Corrections and Rehabilitation [CDCR], 2012). As a result of the increase in the inmate population and decrease in available assets to fund the facilities, California created a policy that deviated significantly from previous policies. The new idea came as the California Summary Parole Initiative, initiated by then Governor Arnold Schwarzenegger (2006).

California Summary Parole Initiative

The California Summary Parole Initiative was a radical rendition of rehabilitation and restoration. This initiative would take offenders who had served most of their sentences behind prison walls and release them up to 20 months before they completed their sentences. Inmates eligible for such treatment were to include "non-violent, non-serious, and non-sex offenders" (Ducheny, 2008, p 3). The definitions of non-violent and non-sex offenders seemed quite apparent on the surface, but quickly became a topic of concern. The meanings of these terms would be defined later by the government, but this was still only the first half of the initiative. The second half was the idea of summary parole. According to the government, summary parole was to be the release of offenders, who qualified for the early release, and parole without the traditional supervision of a parole officer (Ducheny, 2008). Wildermuth (2008) was quick to point out that this initiative also allowed offenders amnesty from parole violations. Individuals would have had to commit new offenses to be carted back to prison.

As one can imagine, there were quite a few problems and concerns raised by California citizens and local governments. Some of the foreseeable problems with the release of up to 22,000 prisoners into society included the following:

- Public safety
- Increased crime
- A precedent
- Job loss

When considering whether to release so many prisoners back into society, the government needed to consider whether the public would be as safe after the releases of the inmates as they were prior to their releases. Increased criminal activity was the second foreseeable problem. There would have been more criminals on the streets and legislatures had no way of knowing whether those criminals would re-offend. As crime increased within a given jurisdiction, the perception of public safety would plummet. Additionally, a precedent would be set. Criminals would walk into their sentencing hearings knowing that the sentences they received would be cut by up to 20 months. This would give the offenders more opportunities to re-offend. Based on the initiative's rationale, many jobs would become unnecessary, once the summary parole took effect. Many parole officers would no longer be required and subsequently would lose their jobs.

Public Safety Realignment Initiative

Given the issues raised by local governments and by activist groups in California, summary parole as proposed in 2008 never materialized. However, that initiative did pave the way for other policies – with equally far-reaching consequences – to be introduced and passed in California. The next initiative would be proposed in 2011 and be referred to as the Public Safety Realignment Initiative (CDCR, 2013). This initiative was the result of the *Brown v. Plata* (2011) United States Supreme Court decision, which found that the State of California had exposed its inmates to cruel and unusual punishment in the form of prison overcrowding. As a result of the U.S. Supreme Court decision along with the Public Safety Realignment

Initiative, control and custody of "lower-level criminal offenders" was transferred from the State to each of the counties (CDCR, 2013, p. i). The individuals who enjoyed the benefits of being released into the custody of the counties were those who were classified as being "non-serious, non-violent, [and] non-sex registrant (non-non-non) offenders" (CDCR, 2013, p. 1). This sounds quite similar to the Summary Parole Initiative mentioned earlier; however, this time, "serious and violent" were defined by the California Penal Code (CDCR, 2013).

The transfers of custody was accompanied by additional funding for inmate supervision. One of the major concerns that drove reducing the prison population was that the State did not have the funds available to build more prisons. As a result of the Public Safety Realignment Initiative, inmates serve their prison sentences in county jails rather than taking up space in the State-run prison system. Additionally, once inmates are released from county facilities, they are supervised by county probation officers, rather than by State parole officers (CDCR, 2012; CDCR, 2013). Therefore, the Public Safety Realignment Initiative provides for some money to be passed down to the counties in order to pay for at least some of the additional workforce that this initiative requires at the county level (CDCR, 2012). The money is meant to assist the counties with costs; however, it is not as much as would have been required if the inmates would have remained in the State system. This helps the State balance its budget.

The Public Safety Realignment Initiative has many lofty and worthy goals. These goals include
- improving the classification system,
- returning inmates to California who have been sent to other states for incarceration,
- improving access to rehabilitation,
- standardizing staffing levels,
- complying with court imposed health care requirements, and
- reducing prison overcrowding (CDCR, 2012).

These goals are all important to the overall success of the initiative. However, the focus here will be on the access to rehabilitative programs, as it directly relates to forensic psychological concerns.

The concept of rehabilitative programs began with a panel of experts making several recommendations about how the rehabilitative process should work. The process included such things as
- assessing risk and need,
- determining the specific programs that should be offered to the offender,
- measuring progress,

- preparing offenders for entry back into society,
- actually reintegrating them, and
- following up with the offenders' post-release (CDCR, 2007a).

One particular aspect of interest to this project was the concept of a re-entry facility that was considered by the State. The concept of a re-entry facility essentially manifests itself as a building placed within a community that blends into its surroundings. In this setting, it teaches individuals who have offended in the past how to avoid offending upon release. This program incorporates such tactics as psychological, cognitive-based strategies and behavior-management tactics. Community support is highly recommended with re-entry and reintegration into society. Above all, a specialized plan is created for each individual who is accepted into the re-entry facility (CDCR, 2007b).

One advantage of the project is the educational factor, which is so important when attempting to reduce recidivism in inmates. When inmates learn valuable and marketable skills, they find it can be easier for them to transition back into a life void of criminal activity. Skills learned in the re-entry program can be directly applied to a position in society. Additional advantages include

- contribution to community businesses,
- less criminal activity, and
- testimonies to the success of the program.

The contributions to the businesses can be found in the inmates working for the businesses, using the skills they learned in the re-entry facility. They are likely to remain in the community where the facility is located because of the community support. Therefore, the community benefits from the trained individuals who come out of the program. There will be less criminal activity because there will be little need for theft or various other activities when a steady job is present that brings in a steady income. After the program has been successful enough to have a population of former inmates in the community, it will be a testament to the program, which will bolster support for the continuation of such a project. Statistics and crime reports will show how the community has benefited from the re-entry facility (CDCR, 2007b).

Some disadvantages of the re-entry facility include

- the possibility that community leaders or members will not be supportive of the initiative,
- local businesses will not want to hire former inmates,
- the programs simply will not work to deter crime, and
- the skills learned in the facility will not be marketable in the community.

Prior to any initiative like this, there is always skepticism within the community. Because of concerns about things like business security and sensitive documents, there is the possibility that local business owners will not want previously convicted criminals to work for their companies. The initiative could be flawed to the point that, though it may not cause additional criminal activity, it may not cause a decrease in criminal activity, which would be very costly to a community. Finally, the skill set learned by the re-entry facility inmates may not be marketable in the community where they reside. Post-release inmates may find themselves quite skilled to do a specific job, but upon searching for a position, learn that all positions have been filled. This may lead to a former inmate having to leave the re-entry community in search of a new community that may or may not be as sympathetic to the needs of the former inmate, resulting in the potential for recidivism (CDCR, 2007b).

Despite the advantages and disadvantages of this initiative, little consideration was initially given to the role that mental·health practitioners should have in the process or to the impact this would have on mental health professionals in the community. The State has made attempts to increase the participation of mental health professionals in the process, but the deficiencies date back to 1991, when Ralph Coleman brought a class-action suit against the State of California (*Coleman v. Brown*, 1995). The issues raised were specific to the State's treatment of mentally ill offenders. Issues included "an inability to identify the seriously mentally ill; inadequate treatment, access to care, and treatment space; and inadequately trained professional staff" (CDCR, 2012, p. 30). These deficiencies have long since been addressed for inmates who are incarcerated. However, these services are not always available for offenders in re-entry programs or offenders who have been released back to the community. Additionally, it has been noted that when a mental health worker is involved in the inmates' treatment long before release is considered, the inmate does significantly better post-release (Farabee, Knight, Garner and Calhoun, 2007).

Mental health professionals can contribute a great deal to re-entry programs. Despite the willingness and capabilities of mental health workers, founders of re-entry programs turn to law enforcement and corrections personnel for advice on how to prepare inmates for re-entry into the community (Fogg, 2006). In the past, inmates usually received psychological services while in prison if there was some reason to suspect mental disorder. Additionally, once inmates were released, few individuals received treatment unless a specific referral had been made by a parole or probation officer (Farabee, 2006).

According to the most recent report from the California Department of Corrections and Rehabilitation (2016), individuals with mental illness are taken a bit more seriously, but, still, some gaps remain in the system. The improvements that have been made to re-entry programs in California include

- substance abuse treatment,
- cognitive-behavioral therapy, and
- pre-employment transition programs (CDCR, 2016).

All of these rehabilitative programs have been included collectively as a technique to reduce recidivism and ultimately, to address, in a meaningful and positive way, the mental health needs of former inmates. Most notably at this point, the mental health needs of former inmates in a re-entry program are "pre-release planning, continuity of care, and linking ex-offenders to public mental health treatment providers in the community" (Davis, 2012, p. 7). With the decentralized prison reform model that the State of California has adopted, these needs are being addressed by only some of the counties in California (Davis, 2012). Improvements need to be made in order to address the remaining issues and to create a more universal best-practice for addressing the needs of offenders.

Conclusion

The State of California, under the Public Safety Realignment Initiative, has made significant strides in providing services to offenders who are incarcerated and also to those in re-entry programs (CDCR, 2016). There is no question that the needs of mentally ill offenders are different than the needs of non-mentally ill offenders (Davis, 2012). Prison reform finds itself in the middle of a debate about the dissemination of treatment services because the mental health profession and the criminal justice system have conflicting goals. Mental health workers are in the business of restoring individuals to the status of fully functioning citizens, while criminal justice professionals are more interested in punishing the offenders. While working within the criminal justice system, mental health workers are sometimes restrained when it comes to helping inmates.

To date, prison policy regarding early release of offenders into re-entry programs has failed the released offenders. Releasing thousands of inmates into local communities must be supported by a strong network of capable and involved mental health workers, both before and after release. If prison reform relating to mental health law continues to be made at all levels of the criminal justice system and not just at the end as inmates are being released back into the community, then the inmate populations will be better served and will be better able to integrate back into society.

Questions for Discussion

1. In what ways might the prison reform conversation look different today had *Brown v. Plata* (2011) not been decided against California?

2. What does summary parole mean for the general public?
3. To what extent is shuffling the inmate population down to the county level actually addressing systemic problems?
4. What role(s) should mental health workers play in the process of rehabilitation while incarcerated, pre-release decision making, and re-entry program support?

References

Brown v. Plata, 563 U.S. 493 (2011).

California Department of Corrections and Rehabilitation. (2007a). Expert panel on adult offender and recidivism reduction programming. Sacramento, CA: California State Government.

California Department of Corrections and Rehabilitation. (2007b). Overview of CDCR Secure Reentry Facility. Sacramento, CA: California State Government.

California Department of Corrections and Rehabilitation. (2012). The future of California Corrections: A blueprint to save billions of dollars, end Federal court oversight and improve the prison system. Retrieved from http://www.cdcr.ca.gov/2012plan/docs/plan/complete.pdf

California Department of Corrections and Rehabilitation. (2013). Realignment report: An examination of offenders released from state prison in the first year of public safety realignment. Retrieved from http://www.cdcr.ca.gov/Adult_Research_Branch/Research_Documents/Realignment_1_Year_Report_12-23-13.pdf

California Department of Corrections and Rehabilitation. (2016). An update to the future of California Corrections. Retrieved from http://www.cdcr.ca.gov/Blueprint-Update-2016/An-Update-to-the-Future-of-California-Corrections-January-2016.pdf

Coleman v. Brown, 912 F. Supp. 1282 (1995).

Davis, A. N. (2012). The effect of realignment on mentally ill offenders. Retrieved from Stanford Law School, Stanford Criminal Justice Center website: http://law.stanford.edu/wp-content/uploads/sites/default/files/child-page/183091/doc/slspublic/Davis_AB109_And_Mentally_Ill_Offenders.pdf

Ducheny, D.M. (2008). Agenda for committee on budget and fiscal review. Sacramento, CA: California State Senate.

Farabee, D. (2006). An evaluation of California's mental health services continuum program for parolees. *Corrections Today, 68*(7), 38-41.

Farabee, D., Knight, K., Garner, B. R. and Calhoun, S. (2007). The inmate prerelease assessment for reentry planning. *Criminal Justice and Behavior, 34*, 1188-1197.

Fogg, S. (2006). Building an offender reentry program: A guide for law enforcement. Washington, D.C.: Bureau of Justice Assistance.

Schwarzenegger, A. (2006). Comprehensive prison reform. Sacramento, CA: California State Government. Retrieved March 8, 2008 from http://gov.ca.gov/index.php?/text/fact-sheet/4966/

Wildermuth, J. (2008, January 12). Prisons: 22,000 prisoners could be set free early to save millions. San Francisco Chronicle. Retrieved March 8, 2008 from http://www.sfgate.com/cgi-bin/article.cgi?file=/c/a/2008/01/12/MNHPUDVP4.DTL

8 JUDICIAL DECISION MAKING

Judicial decision making has been researched for many years by many disciplines (Harrison, 1993; Meyer, 1984; Oliveira, 2007; Stephenson & Staal, 2007). Even though many early decision-making models were based upon mathematical calculations (Uebersax, 1987; Stephenson & Staal, 2007), the review here will be limited to the non-quantitative models of decision making. According to Pennington and Hastie (1992), qualitative models are preferred, because they offer a clearer picture of how decision makers conceptualize and understand material presented. The quantitative models are less reliable in understanding decision making by individuals, but are more reliable in understanding mathematically based decision makers, such as computers.

"The existing decision-making theories and studies from different fields indicate that decision making is a highly complex phenomenon. There is also much conceptual ambiguity in decision making research" (Lauri & Salanterä, 1998, p. 445). This complexity and ambiguity provides for a vast pool of research from which an understanding of decision making can be drawn. The purpose of exploring some of the major theories here is to establish the complexity of decision making and to create a framework for judicial decision-making models that will be discussed later.

Current research, according to Oliveira (2007), places decision-making models into two overarching categories with variations under each:

- Normative decision making
- Descriptive decision making

The categories are based on the nature of the model utilized, and are easily distinguished from each other. A decision-making model is normative if it proposes how decisions ought to be made, and it is descriptive if it proposes some reasoning for how decisions are actually made (Horvitz,

Breese, & Henrion, 1988). This chapter considers each model in more detail.

General Decision-making Models

Normative decision-making models are based upon anecdotal evidence (Oliveira, 2007). They are used in many disciplines, including general management (Harrison, 1993) and hospital management for budgetary considerations (Meyer, 1984). Though normative decision-making theory may be given different names (for example, rational, classical, and clinical), depending on the setting, these names are all under the big umbrella of the normative decision-making theory.

The normative decision-making model assumes that the decision maker has access to all of the necessary costs and benefits regarding competing alternatives to make a complete decision (Kernick & Mannion, 2005). These assumptions include things like knowing all possible outcomes and all possible consequences for those outcomes for the short term at the very least (Oliveira, 2007). "A central tenet of rational decision-making is logical consistency across decisions, regardless of the manner in which available choices are presented" (De Martino, Kumaran, Seymour & Dolan, 2006, p. 684). It has been proposed that, in the event that complete information is unavailable or overly complex, people depend on heuristics or rules of thumb instead of a specific algorithm to come to a final decision (Gilovich, Griffin, & Kahneman, 2002).

According to Oliveira (2007), descriptive model variations include

- schema theory,
- prospect theory, and
- the ambiguity theory.

All of these theories attempt to explain how people actually make decisions across a variety of situations. These are the kinds of decision-making models that best describe the data in the current research.

Schema theory emphasizes the acquisition of new data. When this new data is incompatible with pre-existing beliefs, it may be integrated into one's decision making in the future (Oliveira, 2007). Prospect theory assumes that people make decisions based on probabilities of a certain result from one perspective – failing to take into account all situations, outcomes, and consequences, and thus linking the choice to the outcome. The ambiguity theory, however, links the outcome to a series of choices, based on ever-changing vantage points (Oliveira, 2007).

Additional models that draw on the foundations of normative and descriptive decision-making models are the administrative, incremental, and mixed scanning models (Tarter and Hoy 1998). In the administrative model, decision makers look for a solution that is good enough and remedies the problem. The solution to the problem is a good choice, but not necessarily the best option (Tarter & Hoy, 1998). The incremental model utilizes multiple levels of comparison in order to come to a final conclusion, thereby reducing the number of possible solution alternatives. This model is useful when alternatives or consequences are not clear at the outset of the problem. Here, small steps are made toward the end result, causing incremental change (Tarter & Hoy, 1998).

The mixed scanning model of decision making is one whereby individuals utilize both the administrative and the incremental models. The mixed scanning model is a way to make incremental changes, using solutions that are just good enough, in the hopes that those incremental changes will eventually lead to the best solution (Tarter & Hoy, 1998).

The notion of "processing" is a critical element in cognitive models of decision making (Sharps, Price-Sharps, Day, Nunes, Villagas, & Mitchell, 2005; Sharps, 2003; Sharps, 2010). There are two main approaches to understanding decision making from a cognitive perspective:

- gestalt
- feature-intensive processing (Sharps, 2003)

Gestalt decision making is characterized by a failure to thoroughly consider the costs and benefits of a given activity (Sharps et al., 2005, Sharps, 2003). Feature-intensive processing decision making focuses on the specific costs and benefits of engaging in a given activity (Sharps et al., 2005, Sharps, 2003).

Of all of these models, the ones that best describe the research here are the ones that carry some degree of ambiguity within the respective model. This ambiguity or uncertainty is a result of various aspects of a given case being either unidentified or unable to be substantiated. This ambiguity leads a legal researcher to address several models of decision making that are more in line with the proposed methodology. The previously described models are reconsidered and refined against a criteria known as judicial decision making.

Judicial Decision Making

Just as there "is much conceptual ambiguity in decision making research" generally (Lauri & Salanterä, 1998, p. 445), judicial decision making is "complex, repetitive, and often constrained by information, time, and resources" (Demuth, 2003, p. 880). These constraints can cause as much or more ambiguity in judicial decision making than in general decision making.

Three models of decision making have typically been applied to judges. They include the following:

- Law school model
- Attitudinal model

- Cognitive model (Wrightsman, 1999)

The law school model is not grounded in any of the previously discussed models, but the attitudinal and cognitive models are. It should also be noted that these last two models are related to the descriptive models considered already, not the normative models. Using the framework provided earlier, all three of these models are presented as relating specifically to judicial decision makers.

The first of these models describes the desired format for making decisions as taught in law schools. Law students are taught, from the time they enter law school, to assess the facts and issues in a case and then to compare them with precedent, applicable laws, and state and Federal Constitutional law (Wrightsman, 1999). This is appropriate in the event that all parties agree on the precedent cases, applicable laws, and the pertinent areas of state and Federal Constitutional law. A problem arises when not all judges agree on these three areas. Thus, another means of explaining judicial decision making is required (Wrightsman, 1999).

The alternative model is the attitudinal model (Segal & Spaeth, 2002; Wrightsman, 1999). The attitudinal model does not dismiss the importance of the precedent or the state and Federal Constitutional law, but considers those areas of law as the foundation of the decision-making process on which an individual's attitudes and values are placed (Segal & Spaeth, 2002). The attitudinal model proposes that, if a behavior does not match the judge's ideology, attitudes, values, or all, then the judge will rule against the behavior (Wrightsman, 1999). This is a refined edition of the schema theory; it emphasizes the acquisition of new data (Oliveira, 2007). Per Oliveira (2007), when new data is incompatible with pre-existing beliefs, it may be integrated into one's decision making in the future. However, that aspect is contrary to the assumptions addressed by Wrightsman (1999).

The attitudinal model fell into disfavor somewhat after having not withstood empirical examination (Wrightsman, 1999). Given that the precedent and attitudinal models were not entirely inadequate in explaining judicial decision making, a third model – the cognitive model – has been proposed (Wrightsman, 1999).

The cognitive model takes into consideration the social psychological research regarding how people make decisions. "In the 1930s and 1940s, social psychologists viewed attitudes as strongly predictive of behavior" (Wrightsman, 1999, p. 22). This view has been abandoned mostly but not completely. In a cognitive model, attitudes are still important in that they are believed to filter all cognitions. No longer is there a belief that a cause-and-effect relationship exists between attitudes and decisions; the cognitive social psychological research belittled that belief and emphasized decision making as a process (Wrightsman, 1999).

While these models represent the predominant approaches to

understanding judicial decision making, they are not the only models found in the literature. Some researchers propose actuarial or statistical models to aid judicial decision making (Andrews, Robblee, Saunders, Haurtson, Robinson, Kiessling, & West, 1987; Silver & Chow-Martin, 2002), while others suggest a different cognitive approach that uses "perceptual shorthand" (Steffensmeier, Ulmer, & Kramer, 1998, p. 767). According to Silver and Chow-Martin (2002), "...despite their availability, judges seldom use actuarial (or statistical) prediction tools, but rather rely on perceptual shorthand or intuition" (pp. 561-562).

The use of perceptual shorthand by judicial decision makers (Steffensmeier et al., 1998) can be found when uncertainty regarding future behavior is present, and judicial decision makers attribute stereotypes to the accused, based upon his or her membership(s) in various social categories (Fontaine & Emily, 1978). Similarly, bounded rationality (March & Simon, 1958) is much the same as perceptual shorthand (Steffensmeier et al., 1998) in that it, too, proposes that judicial decision makers draw on past experiences, and also on possible stereotypes and prejudices (Albonetti, 1991). In either theory, the goal is to reduce the amount of uncertainty in the final decision by providing a typical representation of accused individuals who share similar characteristics (Albonetti, 1991; Vigorita, 2003).

Steffensmeier and colleagues (1998) proposed a theory of focal concerns that stems out of the bounded rationality and perceptual shorthand concepts. They proposed that there were three "focal concerns influencing judicial decision making:

- blameworthiness and the degree of harm caused the victim,
- protection of the community, and
- practical implications of sentencing decisions" (Steffensmeier et al., 1998, p. 766).

The first of these focal concerns is the blameworthiness of the offender. The relevant state or Federal law explains the punishment appropriate for an "offender's culpability and the degree of injury caused" (Steffensmeier et al., 1998, p. 766). Blameworthiness and degree of injury to the victim are linked, based upon the possible punishment. Where the punishment is more severe, the offender is assumed to be more culpable and assumed to have caused more harm or injury to the victim. The second concern is that of the protection of the community. This concern is two-fold:

(1) To reduce the risk of violence toward the community.

(2) To deter criminal activity of prospective offenders.

Finally, the third concern is the practical constraints and consequences of the decision. Consequences can range from maintaining a working relationship among the courtroom actors to the defendant's ability to fulfill the sentence for his or her crime.

In addition to the previously mentioned theories of judicial decision making, there is also a body of literature that posits a Biblical view of judicial decision making. A history wrought with Judeo-Christian perspectives and foundations is obvious in the forming of the United States (Barton, 2005), such that "the Bible has been inextricably interwoven into the fabric of American life" (Gaffney, 1986, p. 63). These perspectives and foundations are sprinkled throughout the early documents that separated the United States from England (Barton, 2005; Welch, 2002). "The Bible was nothing short of the underlying fabric upon which American society was founded" (Welch, 2002, p. 619). Given the foundation of the early documents of the United States, a Biblical theory of decision making, specifically judicial decision making, is appropriate.

The Biblical view of judicial decision making is grounded in the scriptural account found in the Holy Bible (Gaffney, 1986). While it is the case that some of the Biblical texts incorporated earlier Near East documents, such the laws of Eshnunna and the Stele with the Law Code of Hammurabi, the Biblical manuscripts corrected and made adaptations appropriate for that time and culture. This means that the individuals in the Biblical account did not pass judgments in a vacuum (Gaffney, 1986). Similarly, judgments in colonial American implemented Biblical concepts, and, at times even, specific scriptural references, although they were sometimes taken out of context (Welch, 2002).

Judgments that were passed against criminals in the Judeo-Christian culture affected the entire community. "Since the covenant [between the people of Israel and God] was struck with the entire people…, there was a strong commitment to communal responsibility for observance of its terms" (Gaffney, 1986, p. 88). According to Gaffney (1986), Moshe Greenberg explained that, if Israel did not punish the offender, God would punish Israel.

The Biblical text prescribed a format for passing judgment upon an accused: the judgment was not to be passed differently for lower-class citizens than for upper-class citizens. "Ye shall have one manner of law, as well for the stranger, as for one of your own country" (Leviticus 24:22, King James Version). However, there was a built-in bias toward those cases that would be heard first during the day – referred to as "benign discriminations" (Gaffney, 1986, p. 91). The intended goal of these discriminations was to ensure that the people who were marginalized by society would not be further marginalized by the judges. These benign discriminations were built into the order of the docket. First, orphans' cases would be heard. Second, widows' cases would be heard. Third, cases brought by women – married or unmarried – would be heard. Finally, cases brought by men would be heard (Gaffney, 1986).

With the exception of the benign discriminations, judges were to be competent and "impartial in the administration of justice" (Gaffney, 1986, p. 91). According to the Bible, a judge should "not respect persons" (Deuteronomy 16: 19, King James Version) such that he or she should give favor to one party or another based on ethnicity/race, age, or sex (Gaffney, 1986, p. 91). Judges were expected to avoid the temptation of bribery by defendants and plaintiffs, unlike the Roman judges (Gaffney, 1986). Partiality was strictly prohibited towards the weak or the powerful, and judges were implored to judge their fellow community members justly (Gaffney, 1986).

Conclusion

Decision making is a psychological phenomenon. In the criminal justice system, there is much power in the hands of the judicial officer sitting at the front of the courtroom. As individuals who are only rarely granted access to participate in the goings-on of the courtroom, it is beneficial to be mindful of the decision-making model employed by the decision maker. Generally, psychologists have worthy insight and information to share in the courtroom setting, but if they cannot convince a judge that their insight is needed and beneficial, the court will never hear it. Finally, the decision-making model employed also provides some insight into the decisions being made by judges.

Questions for Discussion

1. How do Biblical, English, and colonial views of judicial decision making differ from each other?
2. How does having a model structure help understand decisions made by judges?
3. To what extent should Gestalt and feature-intensive decision making be important to the decision maker?
4. With so many models from which to choose, which model is the best model to be used by judges trying to make decisions that affect defendants' lives?

References

Albonetti, C. A. (1991). An integration of theories to explain judicial discretion. *Social Problems, 38*(2), 247-266.

Andrews, D. A., Robblee, M. A., Saunders, R., Haurtson, K., Robinson, D., Kiessling, J. J., & West, D. (1987). Some psychometrics of judicial decision making: Toward a sentencing factors inventory. *Criminal Justice and Behavior, 14*(1), 62-80.

Barton, D. (2005). God: Missing in action from American history. Retrieved from http://www.wallbuilders.com/LIBissuesArticles.asp?id=100

De Martino, B., Kumaran, D., Seymour, B., & Dolan, R. J. (2006). Frames, biases, and rational decision-making in the human brain. *Science, 313*(5787), 684-687.

Demuth, S. (2003). Racial and ethnic differences in pretrial release decision and outcomes: A comparison of Hispanic, Black, and White felony arrestees. *Criminology, 41*(3), 873-907.

Fontaine, G. & Emily, C. (1978). Causal attribution and judicial discretion. *Law and Human Behavior, 2*(4), 323-337.

Gaffney, E. M., Jr. (1986). Biblical law and the first year curriculum of American legal education. *Journal of Law and Religion, 4*(1), 63-95.

Gilovich, T., Griffin, D., & Kahneman, D., (Eds.). (2002). Heuristics and biases: The psychology of intuitive judgment. New York, NY: Cambridge University Press.

Harrison, E. F. (1993). Inter-disciplinary models of decision making. *Management Decision, 21*(8), 27-33.

Horvitz, E. J., Breese, J. S., & Henrion, M. (1988). Decision theory in expert systems and artificial intelligence. *International Journal of Approximate Reasoning, 2*, 247-302.

Kernick, D. & Mannion, R. (2005). Developing an evidence base for intermediate care delivered by GPs with a special interest. *British Journal of General Practice, 55*(521), 908-910.

Lauri, S. & Salanterä, S. (1998). Decision-making models in different fields of nursing. *Research in Nursing and Health, 21*, 443-452.

March, J. & Simon, H. (1958). Organizations. New York, NY: John Wiley & Sons.

Meyer, A. D. (1984). Mingling decision making metaphors. *The Academy of Management Review, 9*, 6-17.

Oliveira, A. (2007). A discussion of rational and psychological decision-making theories and models: The search for a cultural-ethical decision-making model. *Electronic Journal of Business Ethics and Organization Studies, 12*(2), 12-17.

Pennington, N., & Hastie, R. (1992). Explaining the evidence: Tests of the story model for juror decision making. *Journal of Personality and Social Psychology, 62*, 189-206.

Segal, J. A. & Spaeth, H. J. (2002). The Supreme Court and the attitudinal model revisited. New York, NY: Cambridge University Press.

Sharps, M. J. (2003). Aging, representation, and thought: Gestalt and feature-intensive processing. New Brunswick, NJ: Transaction Publishers.

Sharps, M. J. (2010). Processing under pressure: Stress, memory, and decision making in law enforcement. Flushing, NY: Looseleaf Law Publications, Inc.

Sharps, M. J., Price-Sharps, J. L., Day, S. S., Nunes, M. A., Villegas, A. B., & Mitchell, S. (2005). Cognition at risk: Gestalt/feature-intensive processing, attention deficit, and substance abuse. *Current Psychology, 24*(2), 91-101.

Silver, E. & Chow-Martin, L. (2002). A multiple models approach to assessing recidivism risk: Implications for judicial decision making. *Criminal Justice and Behavior, 29*(5), 538-568.

Steffensmeier, D., Ulmer, J., & Kramer, J. (1998). The interaction of race, gender, and age in criminal sentencing: The punishment cost of being young, black, and male. *Criminology, 36*(4), 763-797.

Stephenson, J. A. & Staal, M. A. (2007). An ethical decision-making model for operational psychology. *Ethics and Behavior, 17*(1), 61-82.

Tarter, C. J. & Hoy, W. K. (1998). Toward a contingency theory of decision making. *Journal of Education Administration, 36*(3), 212-228.

Uebersax, J. S. (1987). Diversity of decision-making models and the measurement of interrater agreement. *Psychological Bulletin, 101*(1), 140-146.

Vigorita, M. S. (2003). Judicial risk assessment: The impact of risk, stakes, and jurisdiction. *Criminal Justice Policy Review, 14*(3), 361-376.

Welch, J. W. (2002). Biblical law in America: Historical perspectives and potentials for reform. *Brigham Young University Law Review, 3*, 611-642.

Wrightsman, L. S. (1999). Judicial decision making: Is psychology relevant? New York, NY: Kluwer Academic/Plenum Publishers.

9 VIDEO POLICING AND THE CONSTITUTION

Since the conception of the criminal justice system, criminals have tried for years to outwit law enforcement officers and agencies. Every time local law enforcement catches up with the intellect and technology of the criminals, there seems to be some additional and unexpected advance in the understanding of the criminal that the law enforcement community did not consider. However, despite the advances made by criminals, there are advances in technology that law enforcement has been able to implement that the criminal community is hard pressed to match or surpass. The use of video cameras in communities has become one of the most effective methods of combating the advances made by the criminal community.

Intelligence-gathering techniques have been used in the United States almost as long as it has been an independent nation. Advances have been made, images have become clearer, and efficiency has grown as a result of increased study into technology. The Federal Bureau of Investigation (FBI) is the first agency in the United States to be credited with utilizing video surveillance to apprehend and convict individuals (Nieto, 1997). The late 1960's presented the first United States Congressional law aimed at establishing the appropriate means by which electronic surveillance could be utilized (Omnibus Crime Control and Safe Streets Act of 1968). One of the major and possibly unforeseeable problems with this particular law, enacted in 1968, was that it did not account for and set parameters around video surveillance (Nieto, 1997). Video surveillance became a way to monitor the New York City Municipal Building as early as 1969. Additional cities began similar practices very shortly after New York City (Wilkerson, 2005). The use of electronic surveillance became the norm until the early to middle 1980's, when quality and portability became prevalent.

Rise of Video Policing

However, in the mid 1980's, when video became clearer and more effective, the United States Court of Appeals was asked to consider the constitutionality of such a law. In the case of *United States v. Torres* (1984), Torres was a member of a terrorist group who resided in the United States. Torres had possession of at least two safe houses in which he assembled bombs. Law enforcement investigators, being cognizant of the effective law regarding electronic surveillance, obtained a warrant to video record the safe houses. When the United States (U.S.) Court of Appeals received the case, the issue had already been raised in the lower court regarding the constitutionality of the video recording obtained. The lower court was of the opinion that the video surveillance was in no way different from the other forms of electronic surveillance that was indicated and addressed by the Congressional law of 1968. The U.S. Court of Appeals assessed both sides of the case and ruled that, under the law enacted by Congress in 1968, government entities could use video surveillance to obtain prosecutorial information about individuals and organizations. Additionally, the U.S. Court of Appeals found that, although the 1968 law did not address specifically issues of video surveillance, the principles could be carried over from the auditory information to the visual information (*United States v. Torres*, 1984). Despite the problems in the Congressional law of 1968, the U.S. Court of Appeals was still able to drudge through its language to find the underlying principle that the original authors intended.

Due to the distaste that the case *United States v. Torres* (1984) created, Congress decided to create a privacy act. This Electronic Communications Privacy Act of 1986, "allowed law enforcement to use rapidly expanding technologies such as video surveillance" (Nieto, 1997, p. 3). The goal of this new legislation was to create a balance between the growing need for law enforcement to gather information for the public's well-being and the individual's right to privacy (Nieto, 1997). Congress was quite concerned about the ability of law enforcement to obtain vital information towards the cessation of crime, but they also recognized the rights that are given to every individual under the Fourth Amendment of the U.S. Constitution (Search and Seizure), which establishes that an individual has the right to be secure in his or her person and the possessions thereof (U.S. Const. amend. IV). The Fourth Amendment lists some vague specifics, such as papers and effects, but neglects to mention any particularities, perhaps in an attempt to keep the amendment dynamic and changeable along with the advances in technology.

Initially, video surveillance was conducted using analog systems that were slow and more pixilated than their digital counterparts that evolved in later years. Beginning in the 1980's, a trend quickly took root in mainstream society. Analog closed-circuit cameras were being placed in banks, convenience stores and gas stations as a deterrent to crime; they also became a prosecutorial tool for those thieves that were not deterred by the camera (Wilkerson, 2005). Following the widespread use of analog surveillance came the newest in digital technology that would allow the owner of the cameras to record surveillance video for a month, store it on a hard drive, and access it at a later date in the event of an incident (Wilkerson, 2005). This allowed smaller companies to invest in such a prosecutorial tool because of its affordability as well as its practicability. According to Wilkerson (2005), the video-surveillance industry skyrocketed due to increased demand for the purposes such as individuals keeping tabs on nannies, wives keeping tabs on cheating husbands, and the growing threat of terroristic attacks and other activities aimed at the United States. The internet, like with many other things, has become a catalyst for the surveillance industry. Surveillance can be streamed through an internet connection; the video can be stored at some distant warehouse inside one of many servers and then retrieved over the internet, all in a matter of seconds.

Only within the last fifteen years or so have agencies figured out that so much more policing can be accomplished when video surveillance is incorporated into the mix. Just within the last decade, for example, Fresno police officers explored the possibility of using handheld, wireless devices that would provide them with a better understanding of the situations in which they find themselves. This system of using wireless broadband internet is probably still some time off in the future for day-to-day implementation. However, the IBM Company teamed up with the Fresno Police Department to begin laying the infrastructure to support such a system; this, when implemented, would give officers more portability and more control over the situation they are trained to confront and manage (Kuchinskas, 2005).

In light of all the efforts being made to provide the best in surveillance to law enforcement agencies, leaders in the sales of the video-surveillance-equipment industry, like Bo Larsson, indicate that "[v]ideo surveillance over Internet Protocol is accelerating very fast with numerous law enforcement and public safety agencies across the U.S. adopting wireless video surveillance in order to make their jobs more efficient and cost effective" (Basu, 2007, p. 1-2). According to Cetron and Davies (2008), "[v]ideo surveillance systems have been installed in Chicago; New York City; Washington, D.C.; [and] Tampa, FL" as well as others (p. 46-47).

Just as the Fresno Police Department pushed for the technology back in 2005, they have not slowed in their desire to keep up with the most current advances in technology. In 2015, the Fresno Police Department announced the advent of a real-time crime center (Appleton, 2015; Hoggard, 2015). Essentially, when a 911 call arrives at the Fresno dispatch call center, the call is sent through a program that helps law enforcement have a bit more information about the address to which they are responding (Hoggard, 2015). Some of the information that is provided to law enforcement includes "the threat level, the criminal history of anyone living at the home and a list of known friends and family members" (Appleton, 2015, para. 8). This information is collected from a host of databases and sources, not limited to social media sites and other public information. Despite all of the benefits of using video surveillance and its current prevalence, those who have a growing interest in using it for law enforcement agencies are not without their critics.

Based on historical trends and court rulings, video-surveillance cameras will continue to be an integral aspect of the law enforcement community. Proponents on both sides of the issue are fighting to outdo the other side in hopes that policy will be established specifically for or against the use of video surveillance. Law enforcement and government officials make up the side that is in support of the use of video surveillance. One major organization that is starkly against the use of video surveillance of any kind is the American Civil Liberties Union (ACLU). Both sides have fought vigorously to maintain their positions on the subject. The overwhelming opinion of those in positions to make policy has to be leaning to the side of the law enforcement and government officials, since cameras are continuing to sprout up with increasing speed all over the United States.

However, even with the majority of policy makers in favor of placing video-surveillance cameras in cities and near government buildings, and also tapping into convenience store cameras, there are rational and justifiable reasons why the use of video surveillance should be monitored very closely. First, benefits of the video surveillance system should be considered. Al Maroney, a Fresno Police Department Captain, has direct contact with the video-policing project of his department. Due to his close contact with the project, Maroney (2006) is able to cite several benefits to the video surveillance system. The benefits listed are the identification of repeat offenders and victimizers, as well as provision of a deterrent to criminal activity. Additional benefits to the video-policing tactic include the lack of attention that they draw from the public, the fact that they "never blink" (Maroney, 2006, p. 67), and the provision of a better quality of life for those in a community where the law enforcement personnel are less respected than they should be – which would be the case in most communities.

Video policing and surveillance are a deterrent to crime when communities get involved in the policing aspect. Without the support and vigilance of the community where the cameras are placed, there is little that the law enforcement agencies can do to cease or deter crime. Bucqueroux and Alley (2007) summarized the concept well by explaining that cameras alone are not effective at deterring or ceasing crime, and also community assistance, known as community policing, alone is not effective at deterring or ceasing crime. The fact of the matter is that it is the combination of the two that are proven to be tools that work together well to accomplish the desired outcomes of deterrence and cessation of crime in a given community (Bucqueroux and Alley, 2007). There is little doubt that the community must buy in to the applicability and efficacy of video surveillance. Maroney (2006) indicates that most citizens, when they go out in public, have an expectation of being watched. Most are quite alright with several cameras being placed in the institutions where they conduct their banking. It is a way to ensure that their money is safe. However, it is a little more difficult to foster a perceived need of cameras in a neighborhood where there are people conducting illegal drug trafficking. The reason is that the trafficking of drugs is not as obvious as a bank robbery to most of the community. Additionally, there are some members of a given community who would prefer to deny the existence of such acts, rather than acknowledge them and get them taken care of in an effective way.

Much has been accomplished in recent years that has paved the way for law enforcement agencies to even utilize the technology that is available. The culture has been changed; some say for the worse, and others say for the better. Tolerance has become an increasing phenomenon. Communities and individuals are even positive at times regarding the presence of video surveillance (Dority, 2001). Television is to be held responsible for some of this desensitization. Television shows, such as Cops and Survivor, as well as movies like *The Truman Show* serve to condition the general public to expect video surveillance (Dority, 2001).

When communities are willing to acknowledge criminal activity in their neighborhood and they allow law enforcement officials to implement video surveillance, they gain something far greater than they could have expected. The use of video surveillance in the communities across the United States allows the law enforcement agency force to be multiplied. "Video cameras will extend the vision of [...] existing police officers [... and] will enhance officer safety" (Bucqueroux and Alley, 2007, p. 4). The effectiveness of the video-surveillance cameras has been proven again and again. One such example took place in Philadelphia, Pennsylvania. An individual murdered someone in the early morning hours and the law enforcement agency relied on the video footage to identify the suspect. This led to the suspect being apprehended by the agency. Based on the video footage, this person was also identified as a suspect in an earlier, unsolved murder (Maroney, 2006). The usefulness is irrefutable; however, the rights of individuals are the area of concern for many.

ACLU Concerns

Several problems arise when considering the possibility of placing hundreds, even thousands, of cameras in a given city or area. Some of these problems include the Fourth Amendment rights that all Americans share. Individuals and groups like the ACLU are concerned that the law enforcement and government agencies will "put their noses" in the business of citizens and infringe upon their privacies. As has been seen already, the Fourth Amendment establishes that an individual has the right to be secure in his or her person and the possessions thereof. The ACLU is concerned, and rightfully so, that the use of video surveillance will infringe on the privacy of individuals within their homes, in public places such as school and work, and on the public streets. However, the United States Supreme Court has ruled that anything an individual knowingly exposes to the public, even if it is within a home or workplace, is not protected by the Fourth Amendment (*Smith v. Maryland*, 1979). In contrast, anything an individual attempts to keep private, even if exposed to the public, is protected by the Fourth Amendment (Nieto, 1997). Similarly, "[t]ransactions in plain view in a public forum generally do not raise Fourth Amendment issues" (Nieto, 1997, p. 4). Essentially, any activity performed in public is observable to those around the activity; this includes law enforcement officers', which implies that video surveillance could be used as well.

Though this is a valid concern for the ACLU, there are safeguards put in place that monitor potential risks to privacy infringement. Pixilation is one such method of combating the accusations of privacy infringement. There are programs that applies pixilation when a camera scans a neighborhood and scans right past a resident's window. Pixilation is one of the aspects of a surveillance system that a police department looks for when considering using video cameras in neighborhoods. This being the case for new and more advanced technology, the U.S. Supreme Court, as well as lower courts, have strongly suggested "that within certain limitations, continuous video surveillance is a valid exercise of a state's police powers" (Neito, 1997, p. 5). Obviously, maintenance of public safety is at the forefront of the minds of lawmakers.

Another hindrance to the idea of video policing relates to the ability of the law enforcement agency and the politicians of the community to get the citizens of that community to buy in to the idea of having "big brother" always watching. Typically, individuals are against the idea of "big brother" watching them until "big brother" has a direct impact on catching a criminal who victimized that individual. People do not want a system unless it is directly assisting them with their individual lives. The ACLU is partially responsible for maintaining awareness of the dangers of handing over too much liberty to a governing body. The ACLU asserts that "[a]s technology has improved, so has its ability to infringe on Constitutional rights. Video-surveillance systems are proliferating, despite the fact that they infringe on the freedom of speech and association guaranteed by the

First Amendment" (Schlosberg and Ozer, 2007, p. 6). The contention of the ACLU is that the actions of individuals are much more restricted when they know that someone is watching. Activities that an individual once heartily enjoyed for the sheer purpose of having fun now becomes a perceived suspicious activity and therefore is ceased or done with much caution.

The ACLU is also concerned that policing entities will have increased access to private video surveillance systems through the use of the internet. One city has a program that "gives police Internet access (through a username and password) to live 'feeds' from the video systems of participating businesses" (Schlosberg and Ozer, 2007, p. 7). Additionally, the ACLU is concerned about the security of the video recorded and stored. Systems that use wireless technology are at great risk of being viewed legally or illegally by the public and hacked illegally (Schlosberg and Ozer, 2007). Conditions are just right for any individuals to gain access to wireless surveillance video over the internet. The software is available online, and, despite being encrypted, the transmitted information is still vulnerable (Schlosberg and Ozer, 2007). Similarly, the ACLU has always supported government records being open to the public. This being the case, almost all of the video surveillance recorded and stored would be open to public accessibility (Schlosberg and Ozer, 2007). Having the video surveillance records open to the public, in effect, would work completely against the efforts of the ACLU, making many of the very private acts of the community quite public.

Since the ACLU is so strongly against the use of video surveillance, it has attempted to assess the efficacy of the system. Studies have been conducted to determine if the presence of cameras actually deters crime. Schlosberg and Ozer (2007) cite several studies that indicate no decrease in criminal activity simply because a camera is present. A survey cited by Schlosberg and Ozer (2007) showed that, based on self-reporting data, criminals were more deterred by the number of clerks at a store, an active police patrol, and the number of customers than they were deterred by a video-surveillance system monitoring their every move.

The policy makers of a given community have a difficult duty. They must be able to set aside their personal beliefs and opinions regarding video surveillance, and make laws and policies that are in the best interest of the individuals within the community. The critiquing nature of the ACLU has certainly succeeded in providing a balanced assessment of the issues and concerns. The ACLU makes two recommendations to policy makers of communities considering a video-surveillance system. First, the ACLU recommends that communities evaluate alternative means of keeping their streets safe. Public-safety funds are quite limited and should be put into programs that will return the most for the money put into them. Second, it recommends that communities assess fully a given system's effectiveness and the impact that it may have on its community. An open public forum should be held to allow the community members to voice their opinions regarding any potential impact it may have on them. The ACLU recommends strongly that communities already possessing a fully functioning video-surveillance system reassess the effectiveness of that system, and hold an open public forum where community members can express their opinions and views regarding the system.

Conclusion

Despite attempts made by organizations opposed to the use of video surveillance, there are still those who support wholeheartedly its use and effectiveness. Proponents still maintain that "[v]ideo surveillance cameras may be a viable alternative to increasing the risk of apprehension and diminishing the victimization rate in the higher crime neighborhoods" (Maroney, 2006, p. 71). When criminals decide to commit crimes, they now have to wrestle with the possibilities that their faces will be plastered all over the morning news because of video-surveillance cameras that they missed as they walked into the convenience store the night before.

Questions for Discussion

1. To what extent should the members of a community be allowed to weigh in on whether surveillance cameras should be in their neighborhood?
2. How did *United States v. Torres* change or influence video policing?
3. What are the concerns expressed by the ACLU and are they shared by the general public?
4. How effective is video surveillance at deterring crime?

References

Appleton, R. (2015, July 7). Fresno police unveil state-of-the-art crime tracking system. Retrieved January 19, 2016, from http://www.fresnobee.com/news/local/crime/article26671756.html

Basu, I. (2007). Video surveillance turning smarter with IP-based video cameras. Retrieved May 3, 2008 from http://www.govtech.com/gt/154797?id=&topic=117693&story_pg=3

Bucqueroux, B. and Alley, M. (2007). Cameras and community policing. Lansing City Pulse: September 12, 2007.

Cetron, M. J. and Davies, O. (2008). Trends shaping tomorrow's world. *The Futurist, March/April*, 35-55.

Dority, B. (2001). A brave new world - Or a technological nightmare? Big brother is watching! *The Humanist, May/June*, 9-13.

Electronic Communications Privacy Act of 1986, 18 U.S.C. § 2510.

Hoggard, C. (2015, July 7). Fresno police unveil real time crime center, civil rights advocates worry. Retrieved January 19, 2016, from http://abc30.com/technology/fresno-police-unveil-real-time-crime-center-civil-rights-advocates-worry/834484/

Kuchinskas, S. (2005). Fresno cops to get broadband wireless. Retrieved October 31, 2013 from http://www.internetnews.com/infra/print.php/3496456.

Maroney, A. (2006). Video policing. *Law & Order, 54*(4), 66-71.

Nieto, M. (1997). Public video surveillance: Is it an effective crime prevention tool? Sacramento: California Research Bureau.

Omnibus Crime Control and Safe Streets Act of 1968, 42 U.S.C. § 3711.

Schlosberg, M. and Ozer, N. A. (2007). Under the watchful eye: The proliferation of video surveillance systems in California. San Francisco, CA: Inkworks Press.

Smith v. Maryland, 442 U.S. 735 (1979).

United States v. Torres, 751 F.2d 875 (1984).

U.S. Const. amend. IV.

Wilkerson, L. (2005). The history of video surveillance -- from VCR's to eyes in the sky. Retrieved October 31, 2013 from http://www.video-surveillance-guide.com/history-of-video-surveillance.htm.

10 CALIFORNIA'S SEXUALLY VIOLENT
PREDATOR ACT

Beginning in the 1930s, states began adopting sexual psychopath laws to protect children from a seemingly increasing wave of sexual violence. Driven by high-profile crimes, these laws established guidelines for the civil commitment of sexual offenders who had committed their crimes due to an underlying psychiatric disease or psychopathic personality. Offenders committed under these laws remained in state institutions until they were no longer a threat to public safety. These laws were later discredited, in part, due to the lack of effective treatment options. Most had been repealed by the time the first modern Sexually Violent Predator (SVP) statutes began appearing in the 1990s.

Many key elements of modern SVP statutes are similar to what appeared in the failed sexual psychopath legislation. SVP statutes also provide for the civil commitment of sexually violent predators who, due to an underlying psychiatric condition, pose a threat to the community. The goals, again, are treatment and public safety. However, as with the sexual psychopath laws, concerns over efficacy and legality of these statutes have been raised by the offenders charged under these laws, victims, policy makers, mental health professionals, the legal community, and the general public. One such issue surrounds the constitutionality of civilly committing offenders who have already received sanctions in the criminal justice system. Several key United States Supreme Court cases have considered issues regarding civil commitment (refer to *O'Connor v. Donaldson* [1975], *Parham v. J.R.* [1979], *Addington v. Texas* [1979], *Vitek v. Jones* [1980], *Zinermon v. Burch* [1990]), but the case that specifically addresses issues related to SVP commitments is *Kansas v. Hendricks* (1997). In the *Hendricks* (1997) decision, the U.S. Supreme Court found that the Kansas Sexually Violent Predator Act (1994) met the Constitutional standards for civil commitment; and therefore, the Act did not violate the Due Process, Double Jeopardy, or Ex Post Facto Clauses of the United States Constitution.

The management of sexual offenders is an important policy area for governments across the United States; the State of California is no exception. Two significant pieces of legislation aimed at containing and rehabilitating the state's most dangerous sexual offenders were passed in the 1930s and 1940s. Although later repealed, these early statues, related high-profile cases, and other state and national legislation inspired California's Sexually Violent Predator Act which was passed in 1995. The Act was later amended by Proposition 83, also known as Jessica's Law, in 2006. Despite findings of inefficiencies in the SVP identification process, concerns over effective treatment, and constitutional challenges, California's SVP statute appears to operate within the parameters established by the U.S. Supreme Court.

The Development of Modern Sex Offender Policy

In 1937, three high-profile cases involving the rape and murder of young girls in New York captured local and national attention. The public became acutely interested in sex crimes, leading many to believe that the country was experiencing an increase in sexually-related violence. The public demanded action, causing states to develop new legislation aimed at treating and incarcerating offenders who were deemed "sexual psychopaths" (Hacker & Frym, 1955; Lave, 2009). Michigan passed the first sexual psychopath law in 1935, and other states soon followed. Between 1937 and 1967, 26 states and the District of Columbia had enacted sexual psychopath laws (Lave, 2009). Sexual psychopath laws were characterized by their provisions to civilly commit offenders who had committed sexually-related offenses, due to an underlying psychiatric disorder, disease, or psychopathic personality. The explicit intent of the legislation was to provide these offenders with treatment, and civil commitment was deemed necessary for the health and safety of the general public. Offenders would be kept in confinement until they were "cured" of sexual deviances and no longer dangerous to society.

The California Sexual Psychopath Act was passed in 1939. In California's sexual psychopath law, civil commitment was used in addition to criminal charges. During criminal proceedings, the trial court could suspend the process if there was probable cause for believing the defendant was a sexual psychopath (Hacker & Frym, 1955). The defendant then would be evaluated by at least two psychiatrists, and the findings were reported back to the court. If the judge found the defendant was a sexual psychopath, the defendant would be placed in a psychiatric facility for a 90-day diagnostic and observation period. If hospital staff found that the defendant was not a sexual psychopath, or was a sexual psychopath but would not benefit from treatment, the defendant was returned to the committing court, and criminal proceedings resumed. However, if the hospital staff found that the defendant was a sexual psychopath and could benefit from treatment, the defendant received a commitment hearing (Hacker & Frym, 1955).

Offenders civilly committed under California's Sexual Psychopath Act remained in a state hospital until one of three conditions were met:

- The offender "recovered" and was no longer a "menace" to others.
- The offender was no longer benefiting from treatment and was no longer a "menace" to others.
- The offender had not "recovered" and was still a "menace" to others.

If an offender was found to have met either of the first two provisions, the offender was returned to court and the criminal proceedings resumed at that time (Hacker & Frym, 1955). In some instances, judges would take into consideration the often lengthy periods of time defendants had already spent in state hospitalization as part of their sentencing. In other cases, defendants were then sentenced to state prisons to serve full terms for the criminal charges (Hacker & Frym, 1955). Therefore, offenders who were not part of the treatment process could end up spending less time in state custody than offenders who were receiving treatment.

Even though sexual psychopaths were committed to a treatment setting, little was available in actual treatment. According to Hacker and Frym (1955), "this legislation has neither in practice nor in theory lived up to the high expectations attached to it as its inception" (p. 767). Psychotherapy did not offer much success. The treatment environment was not ideal, as psychotherapy was administered in group settings. Offenders often had to wait until there was space in the groups before they could begin. Some offenders only participated in the Act's provisions as a means of avoiding prison (Hacker & Frym, 1955). One of the biggest flaws with the Act, according to some researchers, was the term "psychopath." The term was no longer in use by psychiatric experts and was too vague. A wide array of behaviors could be considered "psychopathic," from violent rapes of children to non-contact exhibitionism or voyeurism. Some behaviors were noted by researchers to occur in "normal" persons (Hacker & Frym, 1955; Lave, 2009; Sutherland, 1950).

Sexual psychopath laws were later discredited in part due to the lack of effective treatment options and the inability of mental health professionals to identify underlying psychiatric conditions. California's Sexual Psychopath Act (1939) remained in use into the 1970s. By the time the first modern sexually violent predator statute appeared in 1990, nearly all states had repealed these laws (Lave, 2009). Many of the same provisions and problems found in sexual psychopath laws would also appear in later SVP laws.

In 1944, California implemented the Mentally Disordered Sexual Offender (MDSO) statute. The statute allowed offenders whose sexually-related crimes were the result of mental disorders to be placed in a state forensic psychiatric hospital instead of in prison. Offenders had to receive two recommendations from experts in order to begin treatment, and they remained in the hospital until the court determined that they could be sufficiently supervised in an outpatient setting. Outpatient supervision would then continue until it was determined the offender was no longer a danger to others (D'Orazio, Arkowitz, Adams, & Maram, 2009; Dix, 1976). However, implementation of the statute was flawed since offenders discovered they could again serve *less* time by *not* participating in treatment (D'Orazio et al., 2009). This left little incentive for offenders to participate in the program as intended.

In 1969, new California legislation mandated the establishment of 16 county-level treatment facilities. The treatment centers were designed to provide state courts with alternatives to the state forensic psychiatric hospitals for MDSOs. In addition, they were to be used as transition facilities for MDSOs leaving the hospitals and beginning their integration back into communities (D'Orazio et al., 2009). Around 1980, new legislation began that stipulated sexually-related offenders could not live within a mile of a school, which impeded the efforts of these facilities as they were often located in urban areas and, therefore, close to schools (D'Orazio et al., 2009).

Several professional organizations advocated for the repeal of the MDSO law, citing concerns over treatment and a belief that the law was being used as "preventative detention" (D'Orazio et al., 2009, p. 7). Treatment concerns were similar to those raised during the era of the sexual psychopath laws. Knowledge and treatment of sexual offenders had improved since that time, and since the initial passage of the MDSO statute; however, treatment varied considerably by location. Treatment included behavioral therapies, such as aversion therapy, and counter-conditioning. Reality and Family Therapies were also used. In general, during the MDSO period, treatment lacked consistency and was often administered by lower-level treatment staff (D'Orazio et al., 2009). Despite concerns over treatment and its efficacy, major changes would not occur until a high-profile tragedy brought these issues into the public eye.

In 1981, MDSO Theodore Frank was released from a state forensic psychiatric hospital into one of the county-level treatment facilities. Within three months of his release, he kidnapped a two-year-old girl from her front yard and murdered her. Public outcry was immediate, and the legislature quickly determined that the MDSO statute was a "failure." The MDSO statute was repealed effective January 1982. D'Orazio, Arkowitz, Adams, & Maram (2009) report that, as of 2009, a few MDSOs were still in state forensic psychiatric hospitals or in conditional release programs, having already been placed in these institutions prior to the repeal.

During the late 1980s and early 1990s, several high-profile cases involving stranger-child abductions accelerated the movement towards a new era of sex offender policy at the state and national levels. Washington became the first state to implement a new civil commitment law for sexually violent predators as part of a comprehensive sex offender management policy with the 1990 Community Protection Act (Terry & Ackerman, 2009). The Act was a result of a task force, formed by then Governor Booth Gardner in May 1989, following several high-profile cases involving repeat sexual offenders. In May 1987, two years after his release from prison, Earl K. Shriner raped, strangled, and removed the penis from a seven-year-old boy. Over a 24-year period, Shriner had served several prison terms for kidnapping and assault, and although he was never tried due to his diminished mental capacity, he had also been charged with murder. While in custody, Shriner freely admitted his intentions to torture children after his release. Officials had attempted to commit him under the state's existing civil commitment laws without success (Boerner, 1992; Lieb, 1996; Maleng, 1992; Terry & Ackerman, 2009; Watkins Anderson & Masters, 1992).

Diane Ballasiotes, a young Seattle business woman, was kidnapped and murdered by an inmate on work release who had a history of violent sexual offenses. Gene Raymond Kane had served 13 years for previously attacking two women. Kane had also been considered for civil commitment under Washington's sexual psychopathy program, but the hospital considered him "too dangerous to handle" (Boerner, 1992; Lieb, 1996; Terry & Ackerman, 2009; Watkins Anderson & Masters, 1992). While the Governor's task force was in deliberations, Wesley Allen Dodd was arrested after attempting to kidnap a six-year-old boy from a movie theater in southwest Washington. During the subsequent investigation, he confessed to killing three young boys. Dodd was later executed for his crimes (Boerner, 1992; Lieb, 1996; Terry & Ackerman, 2009).

These cases prompted task force members to suggest several major changes to the way in which sex offenders were processed in the Washington criminal justice system, including:

- increased sentence ranges for all sexual offenses;
- mandatory registration of sex offenders released into the community;
- treatment for offenders;
- compensation for victims; and

- provisions for the civil commitment of sexually violent predators (Boerner, 1992; Lieb, 1996; Maleng, 1992).

The SVP statute was developed after determining that existing civil commitment legislation did not adequately address sexual predators. In order for an offender to be considered a sexually violent predator, the offender must have a past history of sexual violence *and* a mental abnormality or personality disorder which made the person likely to engage in predatory acts of sexual violence (Boerner, 1992; Lieb, 1996; Maleng, 1992). The Washington Community Protection Act of 1990 inspired similar legislation at the Federal and state levels, including the development of California's SVP statute (D'Orazio et al., 2009).

Outside of Washington, other high-profile cases were influencing national legislation. In October 1989, 11-year-old Jacob Wetterling was abducted in Minnesota by a stranger, thought to be a repeat sexual offender. The Wetterling case resulted in the Jacob Wetterling Crimes Against Children and Sexually Violent Offender Registration Act, passed by the United States Congress in 1994. The Act required states to establish a system to register and track convicted sex offenders. States that failed to implement the requirement were subject to losing a percentage of Federal funding. In 1994, seven-year-old Megan Kanka was sexually assaulted and murdered by a convicted sex offender after being abducted from her New Jersey home (Levenson, Brannon, Fortney, & Baker, 2007; Terry & Ackerman, 2009). Megan's case prompted New Jersey to enact "Megan's Law," which required community notification as part of sex offender registration. The Federal version of Megan's Law was enacted in 1996 as a subsection of the Wetterling Act. Prior to Megan's Law (1996), community notification of sex offender registrants was at the discretion of law enforcement. After its passage, states were required to make registry information available to the public (Levenson et al., 2007; Terry & Ackerman, 2009).

In 2005, nine-year-old Jessica Lunsford was murdered by a convicted sex offender in Florida, which resulted in the passage of "Jessica's Law." Jessica's Law increased penalties for sex crimes against children and required electronic monitoring for paroled offenders. Other states soon adopted versions of the law and created additional requirements for offenders, such as residency restrictions that restricted sex offenders from living around locations where children tended to gather (Levenson et al., 2007). California's version of the law was adopted in 2006 (D'Orazio et al., 2009). These high-profile crimes were happening as changes occurred in California's civil commitment statute for violent sexual offenders and are important for understanding the current SVP statute.

In 1995, the California legislature passed the Sexually Violent Predator Act. To be classified as an SVP in California, an offender had to have been convicted of a sexually violent offense and to have a diagnosed mental disorder which made the offender likely to commit future sexually violent offenses. The Act was immediately opposed by mental health and justice organizations. The American Psychiatric Association testified during the legislative hearings that there was "no known treatment for a number of these predators" (qtd. in D'Orazio et al., 2009, p. 14). Experts in the field were concerned that the true intention of the Act was continued incarceration – not treatment (Barvir, 2008; D'Orazio et al., 2009).

Proposition 83, California's version of Jessica's Law, was passed by more than 70% of voters in 2006. As a result of Proposition 83, the existing SVP statute was amended in several important ways:

- First, prior to Jessica's Law, offenders had to have more than one victim before they received an SVP assessment. After its passage, only one victim was needed to classify an offender as a sexually violent predator (D'Orazio et al., 2009).
- Second, before Jessica's Law, only nine offenses could prompt an SVP assessment; after, that number increased to 34.
- Third, Jessica's Law increased the number of sex crimes in the California Penal Code, lengthened minimum sentences, and extended parole terms.
- Finally, Jessica's Law allows for SVPs to be held *indefinitely*, whereas previous law only allowed for a commitment period of two years (Barvir, 2008; D'Orazio et al., 2009).

In addition to the changes made to the SVP statute, Jessica's Law also mandated lifetime Global Positioning System (GPS) monitoring for registered sex offenders and prohibition of offenders from living within 2,000 feet of a school or park (D'Orazio et al., 2009). The residency restriction component of Jessica's Law has undergone numerous legal challenges since its enactment. In a recent challenge, the California Supreme Court ruled that the residency restriction, as applied to registrants in San Diego County, was unconstitutional due to a lack of compliant and affordable housing (refer to *In re Taylor* [2015]).

Problems Associated with SVP Laws

Sex offender management policies, and SVP statutes in particular, are designed to protect the community from dangerous offenders. However, many of these policies assume certain sex offender behaviors that are not supported by empirical research and, thus, may produce unintended results. For example, contrary to what is often believed popularly, sex offenders are not always strangers "lurking in the bushes." Research has found consistently that most offenders are known to victims (California Sex Offender Management Board [CASOMB], 2008; Freeman-Longo, 2000; Levenson et al., 2007). The myth of "stranger danger" may lead to a sense of false security among parents who believe that they are protecting their children by identifying convicted sex offenders, blinding them to the need to educate their children about other situations where sexual assault can occur (Barvir, 2008; CASOMB, 2008; Freeman-Longo, 2000; Levenson et al., 2007). This belief is demonstrated in the legislation that was outlined in the previous section.

Changes in California's SVP statute – resulting from the passage of Jessica's Law – were designed to protect further communities from violent sexual predators. After the implementation of Jessica's Law, the California Department of Mental Health (CDMH) saw a significant increase in the number of referrals for SVP assessments – from 1,850 in 2006 to 8,871 in 2007. However, CDMH did not find a significant increase in the actual number of SVPs. Approximately the same number of offenders that was referred to district attorneys or counsel counsels in 2005 was referred also in 2009 (California State Auditor, 2011). As documented in an inquiry, the California State Auditor (2011) revealed, that between 2007 and 2010, less than one percent of offenders evaluated by CDMH met the criteria for civil commitment. The inquiry also found a number of inefficiencies in the referral process for SVP assessments, namely the lack of pre-screening by staff of the California Department of Corrections and Rehabilitation (CDCR). CDCR staff often referred all offenders who met the basic criteria of the SVP statute, without considering other relevant factors. The increase in referrals was extremely taxing on the CDMH, whom lacked sufficient staff. This resulted in the need to contract a number of assessments to outside providers. In some instances, CDMH concluded that an offender did not meet the criteria of an SVP based upon the opinion of only one assessor, instead of the two required by state law (California State Auditor, 2011).

The cost of housing and treating offenders identified as sexually violent predators is staggering. In an analysis of states that had an SVP program, Gookin (2007) reported that average annual-program-cost was $97,000 per person. According to program estimates from 2006, the cost of an SVP resident per year in California was $166,000, with a total state civil commitment budget of $147.3 million. In contrast, the average cost of a CDCR inmate per year in 2006 was $43,000. In December 2015, the California Sex Offender Management Board (CASOMB; 2016) reported that there were 886 SVPs civilly committed in the state.

Another issue, and arguably the most important, is the efficacy of SVP treatment programs. According to D'Orazio et al. (2009), only 25 to 30 percent of California's SVP commitments and detainees consent to participate in active treatment. Offenders cite a variety of reasons for not participating, from claims of wrongful conviction to beliefs that the treatment program is a "hoax," intended to keep them confined forever (p.

27). The latter point has also been raised by researchers and legal analysts. Miller (2010) highlights the lack of privilege in SVP treatment programs and the use of treatment records in subsequent evaluations for commitment. As part of treatment, offenders admit guilt; discuss their sexual history, possible unreported crimes, and sexual fantasies; and participate in tests of their truth-telling through the use of polygraphs and penile plethysmographs. All treatment records are discoverable, which may be then used against them in commitment proceedings. Offenders are further incentivized against treatment because failures to complete treatment programs are often weighed in favor of commitment, whereas non-participation is considered "neutral." And finally, very few civilly commitment SVPs are ever released from inpatient facilities (CASOMB, 2016; Miller, 2010).

The Hendricks Decision

In *Kansas v. Hendricks* (1997), the U.S. Supreme Court found in favor of the Kansas Sexually Violent Predator (SVP) Act. Like other SVP statutes that had been enacted in other states, Kansas implemented its version of the statute in 1994 after a high-profile case prompted the forming of a task force, which then proposed the Act to the state legislature. In the Kansas version, individuals can be found to be sexually violent predators if three provisions are met:

- First, the individual has committed or has been charged with committing a sexually violent offense.
- Second, the individual has a "mental abnormality" or "personality disorder".
- Third, the individual is likely to commit future sexually violent acts. Individuals found to be SVPs can be held until they are "cured" and no longer a danger to others (*Kansas v. Hendricks*, 1997).

Leroy Hendricks was already serving time in prison when the Act became law and was scheduled to be released in September 1994 to a half-way house. Instead, Kansas petitioned to have Hendricks civilly committed under the new SVP statute. For decades, Hendricks had sexually abused children, spent time in prison, and even spent a little time in treatment programs for sexual offenders. Prison, however, was not a deterrent to Hendricks; during his commitment hearing that is required under the Kansas SVP Act, Hendricks admitted freely that he could not control his behavior when stressed, and that he would continue to harm children (*Kansas v. Hendricks*, 1997). The jury found Hendricks to be an SVP, and he was placed into civil confinement. Hendricks appealed the decision to the Kansas Supreme Court, arguing that the Kansas SVP Act had violated the Due Process, Double Jeopardy, and Ex Post Facto Clauses of the United States Constitution.

The Kansas Supreme Court agreed that the Kansas SVP Act violated Hendricks's due process rights; however, the court did not offer a ruling on the double jeopardy or ex post facto claims. Both Hendricks and the State of Kansas petitioned the U.S. Supreme Court for certiorari, which was granted. In a 5-4 decision, the U.S. Supreme Court reversed the Kansas Supreme Court ruling on the due process violation and further found that the Kansas SVP Act did not violate the Double Jeopardy or Ex Post Facto Clauses of the United States Constitution (*Kansas v. Hendricks*, 1997).

As stated by the United States Court in the *Hendricks* (1997) decision, the Kansas SVP Act did not violate Hendricks's due process rights. It further explained that states have a compelling interest in protecting the public from dangerous persons, and sometimes, this interest may outweigh an individual's right to be free. The U.S. Supreme Court had upheld previously civil commitment statutes that required a finding that the person was mentally ill *and* dangerous. The Kansas SVP Act, in the U.S. Supreme Court's opinion, met these requirements. The Kansas SVP Act stipulated clearly that an individual must have a mental abnormality or personality disorder *and* be likely to commit future violent acts. The U.S. Supreme Court found further that, since the provisions under the Kansas SVP Act are civil and not criminal, and, therefore, not punitive, the Act did not violate the Double Jeopardy or Ex Post Facto Clauses.

To determine whether a law is criminal or civil, the U.S. Supreme Court established a seven-factor test in *Kennedy v. Mendoza-Martinez* (1963). The seven factors are as follows:

- [...] whether the sanction involves an affirmative disability or restraint
- whether it has historically been regarded as a punishment;
- whether it comes into play only on a finding of scienter;
- whether its operation will promote the traditional aims of punishment, retribution and deterrence;
- whether the behavior to which it applies is already a crime;
- whether an alternative purpose to which it may rationally be connected is assignable for it; and
- whether it appears excessive in relation to the alternative purpose assigned (*Kennedy v. Mendoza-Martinez*, 1963).

In line with the *Kennedy v. Mendoza-Martinez* (1963) factors, the U.S. Supreme Court outlined several conclusions in the *Hendricks* (1997) decision that would support a finding that implementation of the Kansas SVP Act was intended to be a civil process:

1. Although, the Kansas SVP Act did allow for affirmative restraint, historically, the commitment of individuals who are dangerously mentally ill has been seen as non-punitive (refer to *United States v.*

Salerno).

2. The Kansas SVP Act lacks a scienter requirement. A finding of scienter is required in criminal statutes, and the U.S. Supreme Court found the absence of such a requirement is more evident of the legislature's intent.

3. The Kansas SVP Act does not promote the traditional aims of punishment. The Act is not retributive, as a criminal conviction is not required for commitment. Information on prior offenses is used, not to punish, but to determine the existence of a mental illness or future dangerousness. And, the Kansas SVP Act does not serve as a deterrent, for, according to the U.S. Supreme Court, individuals who have a mental abnormality or a personality disorder are unlikely to be deterred by the threat of civil confinement.

4. The legislature intended for the Kansas SVP Act to be civil. The petitioner has the burden of proof to demonstrate, that, while intended as civil, a law may actually be punitive, therefore negating the intent of the legislature. Hendricks, according to the U.S. Supreme Court, did not satisfy the level of proof necessary to support this finding.

5. The length of conferment is not tied to punishment. Individuals are held until their mental abnormalities no longer make them threats to others. SVPs held in confinement are entitled to a hearing on a yearly basis.

6. Finally, according to the U.S. Supreme Court, absence of treatment does not make the Kansas SVP Act punitive. Hendricks argued that the Act failed to offer legitimate treatment, thereby making confinement actually punitive. The U.S. Supreme Court disagreed with that premise, stating the lack of treatment does not mean an individual cannot be civilly confined. Persons may be quarantined involuntarily in cases of contagious physical illnesses that pose serious risks to the public. The U.S. Constitution does not bar civilly confining someone with a severe mental illness just because the illness is not treatable or because the confinement does not offer a "cure." The U.S. Supreme Court acknowledged further that Hendricks was the first person held under the new statute, and the State may not have been prepared for treatment. The State of Kansas testified at the U.S. Supreme Court hearing that, at the time, SVPs were receiving upwards of 30 hours of treatment per week (*Kansas v. Hendricks*, 1997).

Other analysts, however, believe that the U.S. Supreme Court's decision was flawed, and that the Kansas SVP Act is unconstitutional. According to Rollman (1998), the Act fails to require a finding of mental illness. Rollman (1998) addresses the U.S. Supreme Court's finding that the "mental abnormality" language in the Kansas SVP Act essentially means the same thing as "mental illness," and, therefore, meets the requirement that the statute require a finding of mental illness *and* future dangerousness. Comparison between the language used in the Kansas SVP Act to the language used in the State's general civil commitment statute, in his opinion, is evidence that the Act does not require a finding of mental illness. The Kansas legislature, therefore, created the Kansas SVP Act to address these individuals who were not mentally ill.

One of the issues cited by the dissent in the *Hendricks* (1997) decision was the lack of treatment. According to the majority opinion, lack of effective treatment does not make the Kansas SVP Act punitive automatically. However, the dissent considered treatment as an essential component to civil commitment, especially since one of the commitment criteria was the finding of a mental illness. Without treatment, the minority opinion found that the Kansas SVP Act was nothing more than punishment under a different name. For these reasons, the U.S. Supreme Court may have found just as easily that the Kansas SVP Act is truly punitive, and, therefore, subject to double jeopardy and ex post facto considerations.

When Civil Sanctions Become Punitive

As outlined the *Hendricks* (1997) decision, the intent of the legislature is an important factor when considering whether the SVP laws are civil or criminal in nature. Courts have found that, in certain cases, despite having a civil label, civil sanctions could constitute punishment and would, therefore, be unconstitutional under the Fifth Amendment. An example of this can be found in *United States. v. Halper* (1989). In the *Halper* (1989) case, the Federal government sought a civil action under the False Claims Act (21 U.S.C. §§3729-3731) against the respondent. The respondent had been convicted previously on 65 counts of submitting false claims and was sentenced to two years in prison and a $5,000 fine. The total amount the respondent had defrauded the government was $585, yet the amount that could have been awarded in the civil proceedings was $130,000 ($2,000 for each of the 65 total counts).

Believing that a $130,000 fine would constitute double jeopardy since the respondent had already received a criminal sentence, and the total amount was 220 times the government's actual damages, the United States District Court instead entered a summary judgment on behalf of the government for $16,000 (*United States v. Halper*, 1989). The government appealed, but the U.S. Supreme Court held that:

> [...] under the Double Jeopardy Clause a defendant who already has been punished in a criminal prosecution may not be subjected to an

additional civil sanction to the extent that the second sanction may not fairly be characterized as remedial, but only as a deterrent or retribution. (*United States v. Halper*, 1989)

The U.S. Supreme Court found that a $130,000 fine was greatly disproportionate to the government's actual damages, and would, thereby, make such a fine a second punishment. The U.S. Supreme Court further commented that, although there could be instances when a civil sanction could be so disproportionate as to constitute punishment, the government is still entitled to seek civil damages. In *Halper* (1989), the justices found that, in cases where an individual has not been punished previously, even if the civil sanction is punitive, double jeopardy would not apply.

A statement in the *Halper* (1989) opinion seems to set the stage for a comparative discussion of the differences between the decisions in *Halper* (which was cited in the *Hendricks* dissent) and *Hendricks* (1997):

[…] this rule of reason is a rule for the rare case in which a fixed-penalty provision subjects a prolific but small-gauge offender to a sanction overwhelmingly disproportionate to the damages he or she has caused. (*United States v. Halper*, 1989)

Sexually violent offenders would most likely fall outside of the "small-gauge offender" in the eyes of most individuals, and placing a value on safety and on the pain of victims is difficult. In that regard, in the case of SVP commitments, demonstrating a disproportionate sanction would be nearly impossible.

Courts have considered other cases regarding disproportionate civil sanctions, but they fall primarily in cases of forfeiture and fines. Since *Halper* (1989), similar issues have been heard in several cases: In *United States v. Ursery* (1996), the U.S. Government challenged an appellate court ruling that the Fifth Amendment prohibited the U.S. Government from seeking criminal prosecution and civil property forfeiture for the same offense. The U.S. Supreme Court reversed the appellate court's ruling. While the U.S. Supreme Court did consider the issue that such forfeitures could be punitive, it ruled ultimately that forfeitures were not subject to double jeopardy.

In *Austin v. United States* (1993), the respondent had pled guilty previously to possession of cocaine with intent to distribute but was appealing the forfeiture of his mobile home and auto-body shop. Although the respondent was asking the U.S. Supreme Court to decide whether the government's actions were criminal or civil or nature, the United State Supreme Court believed that the true question was whether the government's intended action was punitive. The U.S. Supreme Court reversed and remanded the decision, ultimately finding that the forfeiture was intended to punish. The respondent had also asked the U.S. Supreme Court to consider establishing a "test" to be used when determining whether a forfeiture was excessive, but the U.S. Supreme Court declined, instead allowing lower courts to consider that issue.

Conclusion

Although the *Halper* (1989) decision found that civil sanctions may constitute punishment in situations where the action is resulting from the same behavior that had already been subject to criminal sanctions, subsequent decisions have found circumstances where actions resulting from the same offense are permitted. When considering such cases, the issues appear to be whether the action is considered punishment, whether the action is considered excessive, or both. When applying these standards to SVP statutes, making such distinctions may be difficult. Confining an individual against his or her will could certainly be considered punishment, but the United States has a long history of civilly committing individuals under the objective of treatment. Taking away an individual's liberty should not be considered lightly, but is it excessive compared to the lives of potential victims?

California's SVP Act will remain as long as civil commitment is non-punitive in the eyes of the court. But considering the history of sex offender legislation in the United States, public support seems to rise and fall, depending on success of such legislation and also on occurrences of high-profile cases. SVP laws may find themselves challenged in other areas, such as costs and treatment outcomes, long before they are subjected to changes in the courts.

Questions for Discussion

1. What is the distinction between sexual offenders and sexually violent predators? To what extent should they be treated differently?
2. To what extent should the correctional system attempt to rehabilitate violent sexual offenders?
3. How does Jessica's Law (1996) differ from Megan's Law (2006)?
4. What benefits exist for a defendant if a case is deemed a civil matter? What benefits exist for a victim if a case is deemed a criminal matter?

References

Austin v. United States, 509 U.S. 602 (1993).

Barvir, A. (2008). When hysteria and good intentions collide: Constitutional considerations of California's Sexual Predator Punishment and Control Act. *Whittier Law Review, 29*(3), 679-706.

Boerner, D. (1992). Confronting violence: In the act and in the word. *Seattle University Law Review, 15*(3), 525-577. Retrieved from http://digitalcommons.law.seattleu.edu/sulr/vol15/iss3/3/

California Sex Offender Management Board. (2008, January). *An assessment of current management practices of adult sex offenders in California: Initial report.* Retrieved from http://www.casomb.org/ docs/sombreport1.pdf

California Sex Offender Management Board. (2016, February). *Year end report 2015.* Retrieved from http://www.casomb.org/docs/CASOMB_End-of-Year-Report_2015.pdf

California State Auditor. (2011). *Sex offender commitment program: Streamlining the process for identifying potential sexually violent predators would reduce unnecessary or duplicative work* (Report 2010-116). Retrieved from https://www.bsa.ca.gov/pdfs/reports/2010-116.pdf

California Mentally Disordered Sexual Offender, Cal Wel & Inst Code §§6300-6331 (1944).

California Proposition 83, Jessica's Law, Cal Pen Code § 3003.5 (2006).

California Sexual Psychopath Act, Cal Wel & Inst Code §§5500-5516 (1939)

California Sexually Violent Predator Act, Cal Wel & Inst Code § 6600 et seq. (1995).

D'Orazio, D.M., Arkowitz, S., Adams, J., & Maram, W. (2009). *The California sexually violent predator statute: History, description & areas for improvement.* Retrieved from the California Coalition on Sexual Offending website: https://ccoso.org/sites/default/files/CCOSO%20SVP%20Paper.pdf

Dix, G.E. (1976). Differential processing of abnormal sex offenders: Utilization of California's mentally disordered sex offender program. *Journal of Criminal Law and Criminology, 67*(2), 233-243. Retrieved from http://scholarlycommons.law.northwestern.edu/cgi/viewcontent.cgi?article= 5981&context=jclc

False Claims Act (FCA), 21 U.S.C. §§3729-3731

Freeman-Longo, R. (2000). *Myths and facts about sex offenders.* Retrieved from Center for Sex Offender Management website: http://www.csom.org/pubs/mythsfacts.pdf

Gookin, K. (2007). *Comparison of state laws authorizing involuntary commitment of sexually violent predators: 2006 update, revised* (Document No. 07-08-1101). Retrieved from Washington State Institute for Public Policy website: http://www.wsipp.wa.gov/ReportFile/989/Wsipp_Comparison-of-State-Laws-Authorizing-Involuntary-Commitment-of-Sexually-Violent-Predators-2006-Update-Revised_Full-Report.pdf

Hacker, F.J., & Frym, M. (1955). The sexual psychopath in practice: A critical discussion. *California Law Review, 43*(5), 766-780. doi:10.15779/Z386J4T

Jacob Wetterling Crimes Against Children and Sexually Violent Offender Registration Act, 42 U.S.C. § 14071 (1994).

Kansas Sexually Violent Predator Act, Kan. Stat. Ann. § 59-29a01 et seq. (1994).

Kansas v. Hendricks, 521 U.S. 346 (1997).

Kennedy v. Mendoza-Martinez, 372 U.S. 144 (1963).

Lave, T.R. (2009). Only yesterday: The rise and fall of twentieth century sexual psychopath laws. *Louisiana Law Review, 69*(3), 549-591. Retrieved from http://digitalcommons.law.lsu.edu/lalrev/vol69/iss3/3

Levenson, J.S., Brannon, Y.N., Fortney, T., & Baker, J. (2007). Public perceptions about sex offenders and community protection policies. *Analyses of Social Issues and Public Policy, 7*(1), 137-161. doi: 10.1111/j.1530-2415.2007.00119.x

Lieb, R. (1996). *Washington's sexually predator law: Legislative history and comparisons with other states* (Document No. 96-12-1101). Retrieved from Washington State Institute for Public Policy website: http://www.wsipp.wa.gov/ReportFile/1244/Wsipp_Washingtons-Sexually-Violent-Predator-Law-Legislative-History-and-Comparisons-With-Other-States_Full-Report.pdf

Maleng, N. (1992). The Community Protection Act and the Sexually Violent Predator Statute. *Seattle University Law Review, 15*(3), 821-826. Retrieved from http://digitalcommons.law.seattleu.edu/sulr/vol15/iss3/12/

Megan's Law, 42 U.S.C. § 14071(e) (1996).

Miller, J.A. (2010). Sex offender civil commitment: The treatment paradox. *California Law Review, 98*(6), 2093-2128. doi:10.15779/Z38HD82

Rollman, E.M. (1998). Supreme Court review: "Mental illness": A sexually violent predator is punished twice for one crime. *Journal of Criminal Law and Criminology, 88*(3), 985-1014. Retrieved from http://scholarlycommons.law.northwestern.edu/cgi/viewcontent.cgi?article=6966 &context=jclc

Sutherland, E.H. (1950). The sexual psychopath laws. *Journal of Criminal Law and Criminology, 40*(5), 543-554. Retrieved from http://scholarlycommons.law.northwestern.edu/cgi/viewcontent.cgi?article=3714&context=jclc

Terry, K.J., & Ackerman, A.R. (2009). A brief history of major sex offender laws. In R.G. Wright (Ed.), *Sex offender laws: failed policies, new directions* (pp. 65-98). New York: Springer Publishing Company, Inc.

United States v. Halper, 490 U.S. 435 (1989).

United States v. Ursery, 518 U.S. 267 (1996).

Washington Community Protection Act of 1990, Sexually Violent Predators, RCW § 71.09

Watkins Anderson, N. & Masters, K.W. (Eds.). (1992). Editor's preface: Predators and politics: The dichotomies of translation in the Washington Sexually Violent Predators Statute [Special section]. *Seattle*

University Law Review, 15(3), 507-515. Retrieved from http://digitalcommons. law.seattleu.edu/sulr/vol15/iss3/1/

11 BEHAVIORAL ASSUMPTIONS REGARDING LETHAL INJECTION

An ongoing debate in the United States deals with the constitutionality of the death penalty. Since its inception and implementation, the death penalty has been controversial, but has enjoyed strong support from the Justices of the United States Supreme Court. By examining two recent decisions by the U.S. Supreme Court, the issue of capital punishment by lethal injection will be assessed in an effort to determine some of the possible behavioral assumptions that the U.S. Supreme Court could have made. Similar to U.S. Supreme Court rulings in the past, capital punishment is still upheld as constitutional according to Federal regulations. The behavioral assumptions made by the U.S. Supreme Court are issues that demand assessment from the field of psychology. The results of the assessment should then be provided to the legal system for their implementation.

Since the late 1800's, the U.S. Supreme Court has upheld that capital punishment is constitutional, though there was moratorium placed on capital punishment until sentencing instructions could be more clearly delineated (*Furman v. Georgia*, 1972; *Gregg v. Georgia*, 1976). Scarcely has the U.S. Supreme Court heard or even considered cases regarding such matters as the Constitutionality of the death penalty. However, when specific methods of execution were analyzed, the U.S. Supreme Court upheld the usage of each method unless a more-effective and less-painful method had been researched and proven to be effective. Rulings passed down from the U.S. Supreme Court have emphasized the importance of avoiding the administration of pain simply for the purpose of causing pain (*Baze v. Rees*, 2008). The goal and end result is for the termination of a life, not for the suffering along the way.

Baze v. Rees (2008)

While there is a long list of cases heard by the U.S. Supreme Court on the matter of the death penalty, the analysis here will be with *Baze v. Rees* (2008). The petitioners, Ralph Baze and Thomas Bowling, are both prison inmates on death row in the State of Kentucky. Both men were convicted of a double homicide. The petitioners are of the opinion that, when the executioner performs the execution correctly, the procedure is quite humane. However, their argument is that the Eighth Amendment's ban on cruel and unusual punishment will be violated if the terms of the protocol are not followed properly (U.S. Const. amend. VIII). The inability of the executioner to follow the protocol appropriately would result in a significant amount of pain to the death-row inmate. Therefore, Baze and Bowling petitioned that the three-drug "cocktail" used for lethal injection in the State of Kentucky was cruel and unusual if not mixed properly. The significant amount of pain created by the misjudgment of drugs would cause an inhumane death for the inmate. Conversely, Rees and the State of Kentucky contend that there is no reason to assume that the executioner will get the proportions wrong; thus, there is no reason to assume an inhumane execution.

In the State of Kentucky at that time, a three-drug "cocktail" was used at all lethal-injection executions. The first drug in the cocktail was sodium thiopental, which is a fast-acting sedative that induces a deep, coma-like unconsciousness when given to an individual in the amount used for executions. The second and most recent death penalty case will discuss the use of this sedative in great detail, as it is the subject and foundation of the petitioners claim in that case. The second drug, pancuronium bromide, is a paralytic agent that inhibits all muscular-skeletal movements, including the diaphragm, causing respiration to cease. The third drug, potassium chloride, is used to stimulate a cardiac arrest by interfering with the electrical signals in the body and brain.

It is interesting that the petitioners hung their hats on one drug and not the set of drugs. They are not concerned with the constitutionality of the second and third drugs, but rather, they are concerned primarily about the ability of the executioner to get the first drug administered in the correct dosage to cause the unconscious state adequately.

Baze and Bowling cited two Kentucky State Statutes and one U.S. Constitutional Amendment. The first statute cited by the petitioners was Kentucky Revised Statute 431.220 (1) (a), which generally explains the procedure by which the State will execute death-row inmates. Kentucky Revised Statute 431.220 (1) (a) states that the execution will be conducted by an intravenous injection of a substance or combination of substances that will cause death. This injection will continue until the prisoner is deceased. The purpose of the usage of this statute by the petitioner is to illustrate that the State of Kentucky lays no firm foundation by which execution of an individual should occur; thus, there is significant room for variation and error.

The second statute cited by Baze and Bowling is Kentucky Revised Statute 431.220 (3). This section of the same statute establishes that no physician will be involved in the administration of the necessary drugs to cause death. The physician's involvement in such an act would go against his or her dedication to the Hippocratic Oath as a physician. However, there is a physician present at all executions in the event of a stay of execution or to certify the cause of death when the execution is completed.

Finally, the reason why the U.S. Supreme Court was willing to hear this particular case was because the petitioners claimed that the State of Kentucky was violating the Eighth Amendment to the Constitution (U.S. Const. amend. VIII). This amendment provides for the following:

- All citizens of the United States to be treated humanely and fairly.
- No excessive bail shall be required of an inmate.
- No excessive fines shall be asked from the inmate.
- No cruel and unusual punishment shall be inflicted upon an inmate.

Denno (1997) indicates that the Constitutional relevance to this portion of the Amendment has long been applied to conditions within a prison setting, not the carrying out of an execution. However, the U.S. Supreme Court has found that the cruel and unusual clause of the Eighth Amendment is also applicable to the method and usage of capital punishment, with specific respect to lethal injection.

The U.S. Supreme Court does not have the duty to assess the state's policies and laws with respect to the death penalty. Therefore, the U.S. Supreme Court considered only the potential violation of the Eighth Amendment. With a vote of seven justices to two justices, the decision of the U.S. Supreme Court was largely in favor of Constitutionality of lethal injection as capital punishment. However, despite the overwhelming support of the use of lethal injection, there were six different opinions written for the case. Chief Justice John Roberts wrote the main opinion; four other justices wrote their own concurrences, and Justice Ruth Ginsburg offered a dissent. The divide within the justices' opinions indicates that the U.S. Supreme Court is heartily for the use of the death penalty, but not all in agreement on the reasons to use the death penalty.

In the main opinion, Chief Justice John Roberts provided the rationale behind his decision for the usage of lethal injection. In contrast to the contention that lethal injection could cause a substantial amount of pain if not mixed correctly, the U.S. Supreme Court realized that, because the death penalty is an execution, there is still a risk of pain even when using the most humane means possible. Additionally, the U.S. Constitution does not demand that the risk of all pain be avoided. Isolated events, such as an infrequent mishap by the execution team, do not constitute a substantial risk of serious harm. The risk of undue pain is an exception rather than the rule. In order for the incident to violate the U.S. Constitution, the incident must be a pattern or the rule.

The U.S. Supreme Court contended that the petitioners did not carry their burden of showing the substantial risk involved in utilizing such a method of execution. The U.S. Supreme Court found that the safeguards created by the State of Kentucky were adequate and constitutional. Training and experience are required of those administering the three drugs. The U.S. Supreme Court also refuted the petitioner's contention that a one-drug injection would be sufficient and effective in accomplishing the execution of an inmate. However, the U.S. Supreme Court recognized that this may be the case, but the petitioners provided no proof that this was the case. The concurring Justices, in this case, indicated that neither the Federal government nor any other state may implement a one-drug injection procedure. Additionally, the petitioners were unable to materialize research that created a substantial difference between the effectiveness of the three-drug injection versus a one-drug injection. In conclusion, the U.S. Supreme Court adhered to the principle that "an execution method violates the Eighth Amendment only if it is deliberately designed to inflict pain" (*Baze v. Rees*, 2008, p. 4).

Glossip v. Gross (2015)

The second case and more recent of the two is *Glossip v. Gross* (2015). Much of the initial content describing the history of the support for the death penalty remains the same for this case; however, the interest of the petitioners is somewhat different. In this case, the state of Oklahoma, through a series of circumstances since the *Baze v. Rees* (2008) case, was unable to obtain doses of the first drug in the cocktail, the sodium thiopental. The series of circumstances is a long battle between drug manufacturers and anti-death-penalty advocates. The anti-death-penalty advocates won and caused sodium thiopental and an equivalent, pentobarbital, to be inaccessible to governments in the United States who would use them for lethal injections. To avoid dispute with anti-death penalty advocates (*Glossip v. Gross*, 2015), some drug manufacturers even went so far as to completely cease production of sodium thiopental.

In contrast to the *Baze v. Rees* (2008) case, where the petitioners were concerned with the second and third drugs of the cocktail, the *Glossip v. Gross* (2015) case petitioners are most concerned with the first drug in the cocktail. Due to the shortage of previously acceptable sedatives, a new sedative was employed to accomplish the task – midazolam. This new drug was first used in the State of Florida to execute at least 11 individuals without any notable incidents (*Glossip v. Gross*, 2015). However, when Oklahoma substituted midazolam for the commonly prescribed sedative, issues arose. Somehow, one of the individuals who was to be executed, Clayton Lockett, was able to cut himself twice at the bend of the elbow, making it abundantly difficult to establish an intravenous access point (IV) in the arm. As a result, an IV was established in a femoral artery in one of his legs. Partially through the execution, the attending medical staff realized that the femoral IV was not set properly. The execution was ceased upon realization, but the condemned man died shortly thereafter (*Glossip v. Gross*, 2015).

The legal issue that surrounds this case, which was the reason the U.S. Supreme Court heard the case, was again the Eighth Amendment to the U.S. Constitution. However, just like in the *Baze v. Rees* (2008) case, the U.S. Supreme Court found that the petitioners did not provide sufficient evidence for their claims: that Oklahoma's substitution of midazolam was unconstitutional because it presented a substantial risk of needless harm or injury. The majority opinion, written by Justice Samuel Alito, cited several aspects of the petitioner's case where issues existed. One such concern, raised by Justice Samuel Alito, draws attention to a bit of precedent citing "numerous courts have concluded that the use of midazolam as the first drug […] is likely to render an inmate insensate to pain" (*Glossip v. Gross*, 2015, p. 17). Midazolam's ability to render the painful effects of the second and third drug was affirmed, by two separate lower courts, and thus, would not be overturned lightly by the Justices in the *Glossip v. Gross* (2015) case.

Similarly, Justice Samuel Alito recognized that the State of Oklahoma had taken steps to protect against any further mishaps like the one that occurred with Clayton Lockett. These precautions included three safeguard requirements, which can also be found as dissenting remarks in the *Baze v. Rees* (2008) case, that indicated some level of due process on the part of Oklahoma officials. The three safeguards are as follows:

1. The creation of a primary IV and a secondary IV
2. Confirmation of the viability of each IV
3. The monitoring of the level of consciousness at all times during the execution (*Glossip v. Gross*, 2015)

As far as the majority opinion of U.S. Supreme Court is concerned, Oklahoma officials have done their due diligence in providing the most humane and Constitutional execution of the death penalty.

Analysis of Behavioral Assumptions

In any court system, there is sometimes a lack of understanding with respect to the psychological aspects of the legal system, such as the understanding of human behavior and the psychological impacts of certain types of punishment. Those psychological aspects give way to behavioral assumptions. The problem with these assumptions is that the courts do not realize they are making them. Since the *Glossip v. Gross* (2015) case builds upon the foundation established by the *Baze v. Rees* (2008) case, the behavioral assumptions present in the *Baze v. Rees* (2008) case will be considered first.

Several veterinary doctors submitted a brief to the U.S. Supreme Court regarding the usage of drugs to put domesticated animals to death. The procedure used by veterinary doctors is considered illegal and inhumane if the two latter drugs used by the State of Kentucky are used for the domesticated animals. Pancuronium Bromide and Potassium Chloride are simply not allowed when euthanizing a domesticated animal if the animal is conscious.

The behavioral assumption made by the U.S. Supreme Court is that, though these drugs are not appropriate for veterinarians to utilize, they are appropriate and preferred for a state to utilize in an execution of a person. The trouble, according to Concannon, Geiser, Kerr, Pettifer, and Robertson (2007) is that the first drug, sodium thiopental, is a fast-acting anesthetic that affects the individual quickly but also wears off rapidly. Many problems arise from an insufficient amount of the drug being administered, thereby creating an unconscious state during the administration of the second drug, but maybe not during the administration of the third drug. The point that the veterinary doctors are making is that this set of three drugs may be quite appropriate for usage in the execution setting, but that it must be supervised by a professional who is trained with the drugs being used. If the drugs are being administered by a trained professional, there is less of a chance that the inmate will experience excruciating pain as a result of the administration of the second drug or third drug.

Veterinary professionals assert that the use of the second drug, pancuronium bromide, masks the conscious state of the inmate. The pancuronium bromide is so effective at paralyzing the inmate's voluntary muscles that the inmate can appear unconscious when in fact he or she is quite cognizant of the administration of the second drug, but show no signs of consciousness to the warden or deputy warden in the room with him or her. Since the warden and deputy warden have no medical training, they are unable to assess adequately the inmate's level of consciousness. In contrast, a one-drug concoction of sodium pentobarbital manages to sedate an animal and to accomplish cardiac arrest after a few minutes. This method, however, has not been attempted on human subjects, and has no research backing its effectiveness except in animal subjects (Concannon et al., 2007).

Embedded in the assumption regarding the usage of the three-drug combination is the assumption that the three-drug combination is better than the one drug proposed and utilized by veterinary professions. The U.S. Supreme Court assumes that, just because the three-drug combination has been used in 37 states for a number of years, it is the best method for executing inmates on death row. There is no research to support either side, but the legal system tends to lean to the method that has the most precedent.

The U.S. Supreme Court also fell under the behavioral assumption that those individuals involved in the execution of an inmate have enough integrity and training to get the amount of each drug correct. Though the problem of integrity is a moral one and difficult to test, the problem of adequate training can be tested for efficacy. Kreitzberg and Richter (2007) emphasize that medical doctors are banned from participating in the execution of an inmate, which leaves individuals who are untrained in the medical sciences to proceed with the executions.

Barron and Palombi (2007) underscore four areas in which the lack of training could become a foreseeable issue:

- First, there is a continuation of the execution, despite the inability to achieve a reliable catheter placement.

- Second, unqualified employees decide which of the two intravenous catheters to utilize during the execution.

- Third, since inexperienced employees are pushing the drugs from the syringe to the inmate, there is an increased chance that the untrained individual will cause the intravenous catheter to blow the vein out. This action would cause additional pain to the inmate, above and beyond the pain felt as a result of the administration of the second and third drugs.

- Fourth, in some states, including Kentucky, executions are accomplished by administering each of the drugs through an additional length of tubing (five additional feet) from another room. Due to the additional pressure placed on the syringe, an untrained employee can push too hard on the syringe making it is much easier for the vein to be blown out, as mentioned previously.

Within its protocol, the State of Kentucky Corrections System has a set of checks and balances in place to maintain the appropriate usage of the three-drug injection. Kentucky has repeatedly shown the ability to adapt the procedure they use in lawful lethal injections "when doing so would promote the safe, responsible and humane implementation of the death penalty without creating new risks" (Middendorf & Cummings, 2007, p. 4-5). Kentucky has employed trained and qualified individuals, such as emergency medical technicians and phlebotomists, to perform the intravenous catheters. Additionally, Kentucky trains the execution team numerous times per year so that the process is as humane as possible. "The protocol requires the execution team to practice at least 10 times per calendar year, with each practice to include a complete walk-through of an execution, including the siting of IVs into a volunteer" (Middendorf & Cummings, 2007, p. 12). These procedures would seem to be sufficient, especially since the inmate is expected to die anyway.

Critics indicate that the training provided by Kentucky falls quite short of effective and adequate. The execution team does not practice mixing three grams of the sodium thiopental to the appropriate concentration level. Also, the team does not practice injecting the saline solution into a human body, a step that goes between each of the three drugs (Barron & Palombi, 2007). Similarly, critics believe that "virtually nothing" is done to ensure that the inmate is properly anesthetized (Barron & Palombi, 2007, p. 4). This problem is mostly due to the lack of specialized training it takes to be knowledgeable in the area of anesthesia detection. However, though the arguments from the critics may be valid, they fail to consider the problem of finding a human subject that is willing to die so that the execution team can practice in the most realistic setting – performing all of the necessary components of an execution.

In addition to training and integrity of the executioner, and to the checks and balances in the State of Kentucky, the U.S. Supreme Court has made the behavioral assumption that "cruel," "unusual," or both are achieved only when the method of execution is designed to inflict pain deliberately (*Baze v. Rees*, 2008; *Glossip v. Gross*, 2015). It is certainly a misconception that a governing body is of the opinion that an execution should be painless. The U.S. Supreme Court recognizes, with organizations interested in the cessation of the death penalty, that the Eighth Amendment to the Constitution does not protect against a painless death (Scheidegger, 2007; Middendorf & Cummings, 2007). There will be pain involved in the execution, but the gray area arises when the U.S. Supreme Court has to decide how much pain is too much before it is deemed unconstitutional. Wrapped up in this assumption is another assumption: that the current method of injection – the three-drug combination – is proven scientifically to be effective. Nathan and Green (2007) would contend that the three-drug combination "does not result from scientific or medical study or reasoned consideration of how to implement the method without severe and unnecessary pain and suffering" (p. 5). Regardless of the proven effectiveness of a methodology, the three-drug combination has been utilized for years, and, in the legal terms, that precedent is all that really matters. The three-drug combination has proven effective as far as the U.S. Supreme Court is concerned.

Another assumption is apparent within the *Baze v. Rees* (2008) case and within the body of literature on lethal injection. This assumption is that the Kentucky Department of Corrections was capable of developing the lethal-injection protocols without the benefit of scientific aid or policy oversight. No assistance was provided to those officials setting up the policies and procedures by which executions would be conducted. The only model they had was the Oklahoma model of the three-drug combination (Nathan & Green, 2007; Kreitzberg & Richter, 2007). Without any direction and with the willingness to adapt the original model, the Kentucky Department of Corrections claimed to have taken every precaution foreseeable.

The psychological aspects of the usage of lethal injection are an area that has received little, if any, attention from the psychological sciences. The medical sciences are drawn overwhelmingly to the issue of lethal injection. Understandably, it would be rather difficult and costly to perform research on the psychological trauma experienced by an inmate during an execution, let alone during an execution gone awry. Research on stress and trauma has been conducted, and evidence indicates that everyday stressors can cause trauma to an individual, not to mention the more severe stressors associated with impending death. Perhaps the only relevant way that the trauma of a bad mixture of the three drugs could be studied legitimately is when there is a stay of execution at some point during the administration of either the second or third drug. This would allow physicians to revive the inmate, and also allow psychologists to assess the level of trauma sustained by the inmate as a result of the misadministration of the three drugs.

In a hypothetical case such as this, there is reason to believe that a case of Post-Traumatic Stress Disorder (PTSD) may occur. Some key features of a traumatic event as they relate to PTSD include

- the intensity of the trauma,
- duration for which the person was exposed to the trauma,
- extent of the threat of the trauma, and
- the nature of the trauma (Alloy, Riskind & Manos, 2005).

In the case of a death-penalty execution, all of these factors would be quite effective at inducing stress and trauma. The extent of the threat especially would be very strong, since the end goal was to cause death. However, there are also aspects of the inmate that must be considered. Things such as the previous psychological state of the inmate, his or her coping mechanisms, and the feelings of guilt felt by the inmate are important to recognize and analyze. It is important to note the last of these because of the nature of the event. The inmate is supposed to have worked through all of the details of the reason for execution. However, if there is still some doubt that he or she is guilty of the crime, then a stay of execution, an inappropriate mix of drugs, or both may compound the frustrations of the inmate. Additionally, the recurring memory of the experience may be considered a compounding factor in the mental health of the inmate. All of these factors may contribute to the substantial risk of pain that the U.S. Supreme Court has been attempting to avoid.

An additional behavioral assumption can be seen in the *Glossip v. Gross* (2015) case. This assumption is an assertion, made by the petitioners, that there is no consensus regarding the efficacy of a specific drug, in this case, midazolam. The petitioners cite that only four states use midazolam as the sedative. The assumption here is on both sides. The U.S. Supreme Court Justices assume that the lack of consensus is not sufficient to deem something unacceptable. Conversely, the petitioners assume that the lack of consensus is sufficient to deem something unacceptable despite no evidence to support either side of the argument.

Conclusion

A familiar quotation is raised in the *Glossip v. Gross* (2015) case. Justice Samuel Alito reiterates a concern from the *Baze v. Rees* (2008) case; "allowing a condemned prisoner to challenge a State's execution method merely by showing a slightly or marginally safer alternative [...] would embroil the courts in ongoing scientific controversies beyond their expertise" (*Baze v. Rees*, 2008, syllabus p. 3). This blatantly stated desire to avoid getting caught up in scientific disputes seems interesting, given the preceding behavioral assumptions. Perhaps the U.S. Supreme Court Justices feel as though psychological or behavioral assumptions are not scientific. It could also be that the U.S. Supreme Court Justices are unaware that these behavioral assumptions exist, and count them as legal matters, to be handled at a later date, when the appropriate case arrives at their chambers. Whatever the reason for separating behavioral disputes from scientific disputes, the fact exists that the U.S. Supreme Court recognizes its non-expertise in one area, but not the other.

Despite the dispute regarding whether the death penalty is Constitutional, it is clear that the U.S. Supreme Court Justices agree, although not unanimously, that capital punishment is a necessary aspect of government. The petitioners will not get their stays of execution, but they have managed to challenge some of the behavioral assumptions that the U.S. Supreme Court has held for many years. Much research needs to be done in the area of lethal injection and its psychological effects on the human being. This may be an area that will change the way the Federal government approaches lethal injection and the death penalty as it currently stands.

Questions for Discussion

1. Why do you think most U.S. Supreme Court Justices agree that capital punishment is a necessary aspect of the government?

2. What are some of the reasons why the U.S. Supreme Court Justices make behavioral assumptions?

3. What additional behavioral assumptions exist in *Baze v. Rees* (2008) and *Glossip v. Gross* (2015) cases?

4. What are the moral and ethical implications of utilizing capital punishment?

References

Alloy, L. B., Riskind, J. H. & Manos, M. J. (2005). Abnormal psychology: Current perspectives (9th ed.). New York: McGraw-Hill.

Barron, D.M. & Palombi, J.A. (2007). 2007 U.S. S. Ct. Briefs LEXIS 1994.

Baze v. Rees, 553 U.S. 35 (2008).

Concannon, K., Geiser, D., Kerr, C., Pettifer, G., & Robertson, S. (2007). 2007 U.S. S. Ct. Briefs LEXIS 1480.

Denno, D.W. (1997). Getting to death: Are executions constitutional? *Iowa Law Review, January*. Iowa University.

Furman v. Georgia, 408 U.S. 238 (1972).

Glossip v. Gross, 135 S. Ct. 2726; 576 U.S. _____ (2015).

Gregg v. Georgia, 428 U.S. 153 (1976).

Kentucky Revised Statute 431.220 (1) (a)

Kentucky Revised Statute 431.220 (3)

Kreitzberg, E. & Richter, D. (2007). But can it be fixed? A look at constitutional challenges to lethal injection executions. *Santa Clara Law Review*. Santa Clara University.

Middendorf, J.T. & Cummings, J.C. (2007). U.S. S. Ct. Briefs LEXIS 1877.

Nathan, A.J. & Green, B.A. (2007). U.S. S. Ct. Briefs LEXIS 2012.

Scheidegger, K.S. (2007). 2007 U.S. S. Ct. Briefs LEXIS 1955.

U.S. Const. amend. VIII

12 FORENSIC HYPNOSIS AND ISSUES SURROUNDING TESTIMONY

Hypnosis has been a part of the criminal justice system for more than 150 years. An 1846 State of New York murder trial was the first time hypnotic testimony was admitted as evidence without objection in the United States (Gravitz, 1995; Webert, 2003). Even though this case broke new ground in the use of hypnosis in forensic settings, the courts have continued to view hypnosis with trepidation, and, as in the case of *People v. Ebanks* (1897), have refused to even consider it.

Beginning in the 1960s, hypnotic techniques grew in popularity among police. These techniques were used primarily to enhance incident recall among victims and witnesses. Many in criminal justice believed that hypnosis was capable of enhancing memory or facilitating the retrieval of long-buried, traumatic memories (Fulero & Wrightsman, 2009; Kocsis, 2009). Hypnosis has also been used with criminal suspects. One of the most famous cases of hypnosis in a forensic setting was the Hillside Strangler case. In the late 1970s, the bodies of ten young women were found among the hillsides of Los Angeles. All had been raped and strangled. Kenneth Bianchi was arrested for the murders in 1979, and he began to exhibit signs of multiple personality disorder. Bianchi underwent hypnotic sessions with two trained professionals, and both were convinced of the diagnosis based upon the hypnotic sessions. However, analysis by a third professional revealed that Bianchi's actions under hypnosis were suspect, which led to a conclusion that Bianchi was faking his mental illness and his hypnotic sessions. Due to this revelation, Bianchi pled guilty to several of the murders and was sentenced to life in prison (Fulero & Wrightsman, 2009).

Cases such as Bianchi's illustrate the shortcomings of forensic hypnosis. Questions have been raised regarding the susceptibility of witnesses under hypnosis to develop false memories or to have existing memories. The accuracy or truthfulness of hypnotically enhanced testimony is also a concern. Due to these concerns and others, the practice of forensic hypnosis remains a widely debated issue within the field of psychology. Although some forms of hypnosis have found favor with licensed practitioners as a therapeutic tool, no clear, universal guidelines have been established as to who is qualified to administer hypnosis (Webert, 2003).

Since *People v. Ebanks* (1897), courts have allowed hypnotically enhanced testimony in certain cases. In *State of New Jersey v. Hurd* (1981), the New Jersey Supreme Court found that medical professionals, including psychologists and psychiatrists, can be considered sufficiently qualified to utilize hypnosis in forensic settings. In order to safeguard this process, the Court recommended that a witness's pre-hypnotic testimony be preserved prior to undergoing the procedure. Other courts have found that hypnotically enhanced testimony is inherently unreliable and, therefore, should never be admitted as evidence.

Behavioral Assumptions

Hypnosis is an accepted field of study within psychology. The American Psychological Association (APA) recognizes the study and use of hypnosis in clinical practice. Within APA, there are 54 divisions that have been formed by members to recognize subspecialties or special topics within psychology. APA Division 30, known as the Society of Psychological Hypnosis, is one such division (American Psychological Association, 2016). According to the Division 30 Executive Committee (2014), hypnosis is "a state of consciousness, involving focused attention and reduced peripheral awareness, characterized by an enhanced capacity for response to suggestion" (para. 6). In a therapeutic environment:

> Hypnosis typically involves an introduction to the procedure during which the subject is told that suggestions for imaginative experiences will be presented. The hypnotic induction is an extended initial suggestion for using one's imagination, and may contain further elaborations of the introduction. A hypnotic procedure is used to encourage and evaluate responses to suggestions. When using hypnosis, one person (the subject) is guided by another (the hypnotist) to respond to suggestions for changes in subjective experience, alterations in perception, sensation, emotion, thought or behavior. (Executive Committee of the American Psychological Association, Division of Psychological Hypnosis, 2005)

The goal of the procedure and the nature of the hypnotic process differ among practitioners. Some therapists encourage individuals to relax through suggestion, but this practice is not always necessary. Hypnosis is believed to have been achieved when individuals are responsive to hypnotic suggestions; achievement can also be based upon standardized response scores. Individuals' pre-hypnotic scores can then be used for comparison (Executive Committee of the American Psychological Association, Division of Psychological Hypnosis, 2005).

The relationship between the criminal justice system and the use of hypnosis centers on memory recall, and it is tenuous. Questions are raised about whether the additional information that sometimes surfaces under hypnosis is reliable enough to be used as witness testimony or as an investigative lead. Hypermnesia is an abnormally vivid or complete memory, and the hypnotic hypermnesia effect is the belief that hypnosis may solicit memories that an individual was consciously unable to recall. Research involving eyewitness accounts has consistently demonstrated the tendency for individuals to develop false memories or for victims of traumatic circumstances to be unable to recall details of their experiences (Bartol & Bartol, 2004; Webert, 2003). If the hypnotic hypermnesia effect does exist, hypnosis would provide the criminal justice system with more-reliable witness testimony and more-accurate information that could be used during the course of investigations (Webert, 2003). The courts, in some circumstances, have ascribed to the behavioral assumption that hypnosis can aid in the recall of unconscious memories and can aid in investigations and trial proceedings – with caution. States have also proceeded cautiously with legislation that allows hypnotically refreshed testimony to be admitted during the course of a trial.

Legal Issues

Even though a New York court had previously allowed hypnotically enhanced testimony, the Superior Court of San Diego County, California, denied such testimony in *People v. Ebanks* (1897). Joseph Ebanks was convicted and sentenced to death for the September 1895 murders of Harriet Stiles and her father, J.B. Borden. During the trial, Ebanks called an expert hypnotist as a witness. Ebanks had been hypnotized, and while under that condition, he indicated that he was not guilty of the charges against him. The hypnotist was willing to testify to that affect, but the trial court denied the testimony, stating that "the law of the United States does not recognized hypnotism" (qtd. in *People v. Ebanks*, 1897). On appeal, the Supreme Court of California agreed with the trial court's assessment, stating simply, "the court was right" (*People v. Ebanks*, 1897).

A concurring judge indicated that the California Supreme Court's assessment of hypnotism must be taken in consideration with the case at hand only and not the issue of hypnotism as a whole (*People v. Ebanks*, 1897). Despite this statement, hypnotically affected testimony would generally remain out of the courts for the next seventy years (Webert, 2003).

113

After hypnosis began gaining some credibility in scientific fields, the Court of Special Appeals in Maryland heard a case involving hypnotic testimony in 1968 – *Harding v. State of Maryland*. In this case, the defendant appealed his rape conviction based upon the victim's testimony gathered through hypnosis. Harding had shot the victim, leaving her on the side of the road. Through hypnosis, she was able to recall that Harding later returned to the scene, raped her, and left her in another location, and her testimony was corroborated through evidence.

The Court of Special Appeals affirmed the defendant's conviction based upon the evidence corroborating the victim's testimony, the psychologist's detailed account of hypnosis and the hypnotic process, and the trial court's precautionary instructions regarding hypnosis (*Harding v. State of Maryland*, 1968). In the *Harding* case, the court found hypnotically enhanced testimony was similar to testimony enhanced through other techniques, and such testimony could be challenged through cross-examination (Webert, 2003).

In 1980, the New Jersey Superior Court considered *State of New Jersey v. Hurd*, in which the defendant appealed the trial court's decision to allow testimony given by a witness who had undergone hypnosis. The New Jersey Superior Court granted the defendant's application to preclude the hypnotically enhanced testimony, indicating that the prosecution failed to meet its burden of clear and convincing proof that hypnotically refreshed testimony should be admissible. The prosecution appealed the decision, and the case was heard by the New Jersey Supreme Court. The New Jersey Supreme Court affirmed the appellate court's decision, citing four failures of the prosecution:

1. The hypnotist's knowledge of the case prior to hypnosis was not documented.
2. The witness had not given a statement of memory prior to the hypnosis.
3. The pre-hypnotic session had not been recorded.
4. Representatives from the police department were present during the hypnotic interview.

The court also expressed concerns regarding one of the detective's involvement during the course of the hypnotic session (*State of New Jersey v. Hurd*, 1981). The *Hurd* decision set the standards for the procedural approach to admitting hypnotically obtained testimony, requiring that a qualified psychologist or psychiatrist conduct the session (Webert, 2003; *State of New Jersey v. Hurd*, 1981).

Around the same time, the Supreme Court of Minnesota heard *State of Minnesota v. Mack* (1980). In the *Mack* case, the Minnesota Supreme Court found hypnotically enhanced testimony to be inadmissible in court after highlighting the lack of scientific reliability, in general, and problem areas in the *Mack* case, in particular, including

- the lack of formal education by the hypnotist,
- the purpose of the hypnosis, and
- the length of time between the event and the hypnotic session (*State of Minnesota v. Mack*, 1980).

Further, the Minnesota Supreme Court noted that the victim had remembered things that could not have happened, such as experiencing repeated stabbings, even though medical records only showed one wound, and ordering pizza in a restaurant that did not serve pizza (*State of Minnesota v. Mack*, 1980). The Minnesota Supreme Court cited the standards provided in *Frye v. United States* (1923) in its evaluation of hypnotic testimony. Per the *Frye* rule, testimony regarding the use of a scientific procedure or technique must have general acceptance in its field before it can be admissible in court (1923). Hypnotically enhanced testimony, the court determined, was not generally accepted as scientifically reliable (*State of Minnesota v. Mack*, 1980).

The Supreme Court of California altered its earlier position regarding hypnotically refreshed testimony in *People v. Shirley* (1982), following the decision made in *State of Minnesota v. Mack* (1980). Because of the concerns emerging over the reliability of hypnotic techniques, the Supreme Court of California also adopted a per se rule of inadmissibility (Webert, 2003).

In 1987, the issue regarding the admissibility of hypnotically enhanced testimony reached the U.S. Supreme Court in *Rock v. Arkansas*. In the *Rock v. Arkansas* (1987) case, a domestic dispute ended in the shooting death of the husband. The wife claimed that she could not remember some of the specific details of the event, so the defense opted to pursue hypnosis in order to improve her recall. During the course of the hypnotic session, the defendant remembered that the gun had accidentally discharged and that her hand had not been on the trigger. Subsequent testing of the gun corroborated her hypnotically derived testimony. Despite this, the trial court excluded her hypnotic testimony, and she was sentenced to ten years in prison for manslaughter (*Rock v. Arkansas*, 1987).

The defendant appealed, citing that the exclusion of her testimony violated her Fifth, Sixth, and Fourteenth Amendment rights, but the Arkansas Supreme Court affirmed the trial court's decision. The U.S. Supreme Court found that the decision to exclude her testimony did violate her Fourteenth Amendment due process right to be heard and to offer testimony (U.S. Const. amend. XIV), her Sixth Amendment right to call a witness in her own favor (U.S. Const. amend. VI), and her Fifth Amendment right against self-incrimination (U.S. Const. amend. V), "because the right to testify on one's own behalf was a necessary corollary to that guarantee" (*Rock v. Arkansas*, 1987). The U.S. Supreme Court vacated and remanded the decision, indicating that, although hypnotically aided testimony was controversial, procedural safeguards could protect against its faulty use (*Rock v. Arkansas*, 1987).

Despite the U.S. Supreme Court's decision in *Rock v. Arkansas* (1987), states fall into three categories when considering the admissibility of hypnotically aided testimony:

1. Per se rules of admissibility
2. Per se rules of inadmissibility
3. Case-by case-analysis

It must be noted, however, that any rule that outright prohibits hypnotically aided testimony could be in violation of a defendant's constitutional rights, but the U.S. Supreme Court had held that states are free to develop guidelines for its ufse (Webert, 2003).

The State of California has created guidelines for the use of hypnotically aided testimony, and those can be found in Section 795 of the California Evidence Code. The code indicates that hypnotically aided testimony is not inadmissible as long as the testimony is limited to the matters a witness has recalled and related prior to hypnosis, and the witness's pre-hypnotic memory of the event was recorded. The following procedures also must have been followed:

- A record was made of the witness's pre-hypnotic information as well as any information that was provided to the hypnotist.
- The witness gave informed consent to be hypnotized.
- The session, in its entirety, was videotaped for later review.
- The session was conducted by a licensed medical doctor, psychologist, licensed social worker, or a licensed marriage and family therapist who is experienced in the use of hypnosis and not affiliated with or in the presence of law enforcement, the prosecution, or the defense (California Evidence Code § 795).

Before the testimony can be heard in open court, Section 795 requires a hearing in which the proponent of the hypnotic testimony must prove by clear and convincing evidence that the hypnosis did not alter the witness's recall of pre-hypnotic material, nor will it substantially affect the ability to cross-examine the witness's recall of pre-hypnotic material. During the course of the hearing, both sides have the ability to provide expert testimony and to cross-examine witnesses (California Evidence Code § 795).

Psychological Research

One of the primary issues surrounding hypnosis is its effect on memory. Research has indicated that memories are not simply videotaped storage, as once hypothesized, but are fluid processes, subject to interpretation and suggestibility (French, Garry, & Mori, 2008). Forensic hypnotic interviewing, once popular in the 1980s, has certainly fallen out of favor in the last several years, and the cognitive interview has risen in its place, despite the fact that it employs several hypnotic techniques. Important to note is that not all hypnotic techniques have been dismissed completely by research; evidence has shown that hypnosis may help to produce more accurate memory recall than no memory-facilitation procedures at all (Wagstaff, Cole, Wheatcroft, Marshall, & Barsby, 2007; Wagstaff, Brunas-Wagstaff, Cole & Wheatcroft, 2004). This finding can certainly have practical applications for investigators.

A study completed by Wagstaff and colleagues (2007) found that focused meditation can reliably aid in memory recall for an emotionally salient event with or without context reinstatement. Focused mediation is, essentially, hypnosis without using the term "hypnosis." The belief among researchers is that avoiding the term may reduce the possibility of the inaccurate recall and false-positive confidence that is often associated with hypnosis. Context reinstatement is when participants are asked to describe in detail the situation surrounding the critical event, including their feelings. Context reinstatement has evolved to be part of the cognitive interview, but interestingly enough, has always been a part of the forensic hypnotic interview (Wagstaff et al., 2007). Essentially, modern research has found positive outcomes for hypnotic techniques, but even these are not completely devoid of risk.

Another issue surrounding hypnosis is unwanted side effects of induction, ranging from mild headaches and nausea to psychotic episodes. According to Gruzelier (2000), who reviewed the available literature on hypnotic effects, the likelihood of experiencing ill after-effects varies depending on the individual's hypnotizability and suggestibility, and on the context of the hypnosis. Some individuals are considerably more susceptible to hypnosis than others, and, just as some are more susceptible, others are more likely to develop reactions. Also, considering the context of the hypnosis can affect adverse reactions. Therapeutic hypnosis, especially in conjunction with psychotherapy, can be very intense and also can happen over a considerable period of time. Individual reactions in these situations may differ from those experienced in laboratory situations – involving mostly healthy students – and stage shows, where the context is entertainment as well as personal humiliation (Gruzelier, 2000).

In addition to examinations of hypnotic procedures and effects on memory, researchers have also considered public perceptions of hypnosis, and the impact of those perceptions on the legal system. Fusco & Platania (2011) examined differences in memories recalled without hypnosis and memories recovered with hypnosis in a civil sexual abuse case. Overall, memories recovered through hypnosis were perceived by study participants with greater skepticism, and non-hypnotically enhanced memories were perceived as more credible.

Other researchers, however, have found that hypnotically enhanced testimony is viewed more credible than non-hypnotically enhanced testimony. Wagstaff, Vella, & Perfect (1992), for example, found that mock jurors were more likely to find a defendant guilty when hypnotically enhanced testimony was used. The inconsistent research on public perception of hypnosis, and the perceptions of potential jurors, underscores the need for practitioners in the criminal justice system to remain cautious when considering the use of hypnotically enhanced testimony in the courts.

Conclusion

The current stance of the U.S. Supreme Court, as dictated through *Rock v. Arkansas* (1987), matches the current state of the psychological research surrounding hypnosis – hypnosis cannot be dismissed ultimately, but underlying issues and concerns do exist. More research needs to be conducted into uses, and guidelines surrounding practice need to be created. Modern research has shown the incredibly delicate nature of memory and the ease by which it may be distorted. At the same time, modern hypnotic techniques, masked under a different name, have been found to be of considerable use. The criminal justice system relies heavily on witness and victim statements. As more is learned regarding memory, the likelihood of modern hypnotic techniques finding their way into the court system increases dramatically. States that have not done so already should consider developing legislation for hypnotically enhanced testimony and other memory refreshing techniques, such as focused meditation.

Questions for Discussion

1. What should the qualifications be for individuals permitted to administer hypnosis?
2. Should hypnotically remembered testimony be admissible in court at all?
3. To what extent are the conditions required by the State of California appropriate in allowing for the admissibility of hypnotically remembered testimony?
4. What level of credibility should be given to hypnotically remembered testimony?

References

American Psychological Association. (2016). APA Divisions. Retrieved from http://www.apadivisions.org/
Bartol, C.R., & Bartol, A.M. (2004). *Psychology and the law: Theory, research, and application* (3 ed.). Belmont, California: Wadsworth/Thomson Learning.
California Evidence Code § 795 (2008 FindLaw).

Executive Committee of the American Psychological Association, Division of Psychological Hypnosis. (2005). *New definition: Hypnosis*. Retrieved October 31, 2013, from http://www.apa.org/divisions/div30/define_hypnosis.html

French, L., Garry, M., & Mori, K. (2008). You say tomato?: Collaborative remembering leads to more false memories for intimate couples than for strangers. *Memory, 13*(3), 262-273.

Frye v. United States, 54 App. D.C. 46, 293 F. 1013 (D.C. Cir. 1923).

Fulero, S.M., & Wrightsman, L.S. (2009). *Forensic psychology* (3 ed.). Belmont, California: Wadsworth.

Fusco, A., & Platania, J. (2011). Understanding perceptions of hypnotically recovered memories in the a civil sexual abuse case. *Journal of Forensic Psychology Practice, 11*, 330-350. doi:10.1080/15228932.2011.583908

Gravitz, M.A. (1995). First admission (1846) of hypnotic testimony in court [Abstract]. *American Journal of Clinical Hypnosis, 37*(4). doi: 10.1080/00029157.1995.10403161

Gruzelier, J. (2000). Unwanted effects of hypnosis: A review of the evidence and its implications. *Contemporary Hypnosis, 17*(4), 163-193.

Harding v. State of Maryland, 5 Md. App. 230; 246 A.2d 302; 1968 Md. App. LEXIS 367 (Md. Ct. Spec. App. 1968).

Kocsis, R.N. (Ed.). (2009). *Applied criminal psychology: A guide to forensic behavioral sciences*. Springfield, Illinois: Charles C. Thomas Publisher, LTD.

People v. Ebanks, 117 Cal. 652; 49 P. 1049; 1897 Cal. LEXIS 716 (Cal. 1897).

People v. Shirley, 31 Cal. 3d 18; 723 P.2d 1354; 181 Cal. Rptr. 243; 1982 Cal. LEXIS 157 (Cal. 1982).

Perry, C. (n.d.). Key concepts in hypnosis. *False Memory Syndrome Foundation*. Retrieved October 31, 2013, from http://www.fmsonline.org/hypnosis.html

Rock v. Arkansas, 483 U.S. 44; 107 S. Ct. 2704; 97 L. Ed. 2d 37; 1987 U.S. LEXIS 2732; 55 U.S.L.W. 4925; 22 Fed. R. Evid. Serv. (Callaghan) 1128 (1987).

State of New Jersey v. Hurd, 173 N.J. Super. 333, 414 A.2d 291, 1980 N.J. Super. LEXIS 513 (N.J. Super. Ct. Law Div., 1980).

State of New Jersey v. Hurd, 86 N.J. 525, 432 A.2d 86, 1981 N.J. LEXIS 1654 (1981)

State of Minnesota v. Mack, 31 Cal. 3d 18; 723 P.2d 1354; 181 Cal. Rptr. 243; 1982 Cal. LEXIS 157 (Minn. 1980).

U.S. Const. amend. V

U.S. Const. amend. VI

U.S. Const. amend. XIV

Wagstaff, G., Brunas-Wagstaff, J., Cole, J., & Wheatcroft, J. (2004). New directions in forensic hypnosis: Facilitating memory with a focused mediation technique. *Contemporary Hypnosis, 21*(1), 14-28.

Wagstaff, G.F., Cole, J., Wheatcroft, J., Marshall, M., & Barsby, I. (2007). A componential approach to hypnotic memory facilitation: focused mediation, context reinstatement and eye movements. *Contemporary Hypnosis, 24*(3), 97-108.

Wagstaff, G.F., Vella, M., & Perfect, T. (1992). The effect of hypnotically elicited testimony and jurors' judgments of guilt and innocence. *The Journal of Social Psychology, 132*(5), 591-595.

Webert, D.R.(2003). Are the courts in a trance?: Approaches to the admissibility of hypnotically enhanced witness testimony in light of empirical evidence. *American Criminal Law Review, 40,* 1301-27.

13 EVALUATION OF LEGAL DECISIONS: WOODARD V. JUPITER CHRISTIAN SCHOOL

Often, cases have controversial aspects; especially those which make their way up to the United States Supreme Court. However, some cases are extremely controversial but do not make it all the way to the U.S. Supreme Court. That was the case for *Woodard & Gload v. Jupiter Christian Schools, Inc. & Bellhorn* (2005) (hereinafter, *Woodard v. Jupiter*). The case presented by Woodard allowed the Judges of the Fourth District Court of Appeal of Florida to steal just a bit of the "judicial lime-light." The Florida Impact Law was used as the basis for seeking damages for emotional trauma experienced by Woodard.

Facts of the Case

Jeffery Woodard had attended Jupiter Christian School (hereinafter, Jupiter) for four years. He began his high school career as a freshman at Jupiter; he was a senior at the time of the questioning that precipitated this case. Jupiter is a Bible-centered private school; it is not connected with any established church. However, the school has a chapel on campus, and students are required to attend weekly chapel services.

Jupiter employed Todd Bellhorn as a "Secondary Teacher-HS/Chaplain". As part of his duties, he was expected to minister to high school students and to avail himself to the students as a teacher who could be trusted and approached without fear or intimidation. During Woodard's senior year, Jupiter administrators directed Bellhorn to meet with him to question and counsel him about his sexual orientation. Bellhorn, asking Woodard to leave his class, took him to a private area of the campus.

According to allegations, Bellhorn assured Woodard that their conversation would be kept confidential. Only after receiving this assurance did Woodard divulge his homosexuality. Allegedly, Woodard disclosed this information in order to seek spiritual counsel from Bellhorn, as chaplain, to receive salvation. Bellhorn counseled the student about the Biblical views of homosexuality.

Bellhorn then relayed the content of his conversation with Woodard to the school's administrators, who then disclosed the information to others. The administrators expelled Woodard from Jupiter, based on criticism from the press and the president – equivalent to superintendent – of Jupiter and the rejection of his peers.

Woodard and his mother, Carol Gload, filed a suit against Jupiter and Bellhorn, claiming negligent infliction of emotional distress related to the violation of his duty to keep confidentiality. Jupiter claimed that the information that was provided by Woodard was obtained through a special relationship between Woodard and Bellhorn. Similarly, since, according to the school, Bellhorn was considered a member of clergy, he should be the holder of privilege of the information, which means that he alone should be the custodian of the information without sharing it with anyone else.

Florida statute defines a member of clergy as a priest, rabbi, practitioner of Christian Science, or minister of any religious organization or denomination usually referred to as a church. Furthermore, Florida statute identifies a four-fold test to establish the existence of privilege.

- First, the communication must be made to a member of the clergy.
- Second, the statements made must be for the purpose of seeking spiritual counseling or advice.
- Third, the information must be received during the normal course of the clergy member's practice.
- Fourth, the communication must be made in private with the understanding that it would not be disclosed.

In this case, Florida's impact rule was sought as support for the plaintiff. The impact rule in Florida is a rule designed to assure the validity of claims for emotional distress. The impact rule requires that any emotional distress suffered must stem from the physical injuries caused by an impact before recovery of damages would be awarded to the plaintiff.

Analysis and Implications

There are many U.S. states that have some form of an impact rule. The result of this impact rule makes it impossible for a plaintiff to be compensated for emotional injuries sustained without some form of corresponding physical injury. Going into a trial, many plaintiffs are hopeful that their court will consider their respective cases exceptional. However, much like this case, the opposite is typically true with regard to the impact rule reaching those who have predominately emotional injuries. In the *Woodard v. Jupiter* (2005) case, the U.S. Supreme Court assessed the evidence of both sides and concluded that Jupiter had no liability for the emotional damages sustained by Woodard.

Woodard was having some difficulty reconciling his differences, which is when it was requested that Bellhorn meet with and counsel him regarding some of his concerns. Woodard divulged his sexual orientation only after having the verbal reassurance that the conversation would remain confidential. At a later date, Bellhorn spoke with school administrators about the nature of his conversation with Woodard. The administrators, including the president of the school, moved to expel the student from the school for several reasons. First, Woodard was being harassed by media personnel as well as his classmates. Furthermore, the president of the school also began to make remarks toward Woodard regarding his emotional struggle. Woodard and his mother filed a suit against the school and teacher citing negligence on the part of the teacher and emotional distress that stemmed from his conversations with school administrators.

Florida's Impact Rule Policy

For good reason, Florida has a strict and specific policy for restitution for emotional distress caused by negligence on the part of another individual or group of persons. Wites (n. d.) explains the impact rule as not applicable if, for example, a plaintiff suffers physical injury caused by the emotional distress of witnessing a loved one dying. Specific criteria must be met in order for a plaintiff to receive the benefit of the impact rule:

- First, the plaintiff must have been subjected to some form of physical injury (hence the impact aspect of the rule).
- Second, the plaintiff must exhibit psychological trauma that can be directly linked to the impact in the first criteria.
- Third, the defendant must be involved in some way in the event causing the injury to another.
- Fourth, the defendant must have had a close personal relationship with the individual directly injured.

However, as restrictive as this criteria is, the Supreme Court of Florida has set aside exceptions to the impact rule. In a case involving *Hagan v. Coca-Cola Bottling Co.* (2001), the Florida Supreme Court asserted that they would allow claims for emotional distress in the absence of physical impact, based on ingestion of contaminated food or beverage. Similarly, the Supreme Court of Florida made it clear that allowing recovery for injuries resulting from purely emotional distress would open the flood gates for fictitious claims. This precedent would become a bit of a problem for Woodard due to a lack of physical injury in his case.

The Court's Analysis of the Verdict

Three opinions were included in the original manuscript of the appeal to the Florida Fourth District Court of Appeals. They were provided by: Judge Melanie G. May, Judge Barry J. Stone, and Judge Gary M. Farmer. The opinion carrying the most weight in this case was provided by Judge May. Regarding the outcome of the original case, Judge Stone's opinion concurred with the opinion of Judge May, and Judge Farmer's opinion opposed.

The Opinion of Judge May

Judge May began her analysis by considering the implications of Florida's impact rule against the claims of emotional distress. As mentioned earlier, the reason for the rule is to avoid allowing recovery for injuries resulting from purely emotional distress, as allowing such distress recovery would "open the floodgates" for false claims of emotional distress.

Since the impact rule was created, the Florida Supreme Court has designated several exceptions to the rule. These include the intentional imposition of emotional distress separate from a physical injury. Conversely, the rule excludes certain instances, including attorney negligence, and breach of confidentiality between doctor and patient. Exceptions to the rule have been scarce when the emotional distress outweighs the policy rationale behind the application of the rule.

Woodard claims a special relationship with Bellhorn based on Bellhorn's position of employment at Jupiter, and the allegations that Bellhorn is reasonably believed to be a member of the clergy by students of the school. Though there are several exceptions to the criteria set forth by the Florida Supreme Court, there are currently no exceptions to the impact rule related to the divulgence of confidential information by a member of the clergy. Based on the nature and extent of creating an exception to the rule with regard to clergy, the Florida Fourth District Court of Appeals was unwilling to ignore the impact rule adhered to by the Florida Supreme Court.

The Opinion of Judge Stone

Judge Stone concurred with the majority of Judge May's opinion but addressed the question about the school chaplain by stating that a chaplain is not a member of the clergy. Since Bellhorn would not be considered a member of the clergy, he would not be bound by the same restrictions set forth for clergy members.

The Opinion of Judge Farmer

Judge Farmer disagreed with the judgment to affirm the original decision. The student was confronted and responded to questions raised to him in confidence. That confidence was broken, and the student sued for humiliation and distress.

In the past, cases have been raised that collectively have created a list of inapplicable situations in reference to the impact rule. *Kush v. Lloyd* (1992) established the inapplicability of the impact rule, affirming that predominately emotional damages flowing from an invasion of privacy are recoverable in negligent-defamation cases. In *Gracey v. Eaker* (2002), a psychotherapist disclosed confidential information without authorization, invading the privacy of the plaintiff. In this case, the impact rule was deemed inapplicable and the plaintiffs, a husband and wife, were awarded their claim. *Kush v. Lloyd* (1992) established that damage from emotional distress could be awarded when the distress of the victim is not sufficient to make the impact rule applicable. The same should be true for those cases where damages are more severe.

Based on these cases, Judge Farmer had no doubts about concluding that the impact rule is inapplicable in the case of a psychologist's breach of confidentiality. Therefore, the correlation was presented that the impact rule should not apply to a member of the clergy. Judge Farmer contends that the positions of psychologist and clergy member are similar enough to warrant the same verdict.

The Assumptions of the Impact Rule

The impact rule assumes that the path of human behavior will naturally lead to an overflow of cases based solely on emotional distress. Research does not currently exist that would refute or support such a claim on human behavior. The policy makers of this rule considered a side of human nature that undoubtedly would have been true. However, it is also possible that they missed an opportunity to certify instances in which it would be appropriate to award individuals in certain cases. Similarly, the Florida Fourth District Court of Appeals failed to take into consideration how much the public does or does not know about the law. Assuming that an influx of cases would have been raised based solely on emotional distress assumes that the general public has an uncanny awareness of the current policies and rules and how to abuse them.

For whatever reason, the Florida Supreme Court, in creating this rule, failed to consider the ability for psychologists to assess the validity of emotional distress. The court took it upon itself to assess the mental status and extent of damages, though no prior education or knowledge of the assessment of such emotional distress had been acquired. In the construction of this policy, lawmakers made the assumption that fictitious or speculative claims of emotional distress could not be reconciled by the tools of assessment at the fingertips of psychological professionals.

Conclusion

The impact rule's creation, the subsequent exceptions that have been recognized, and the exceptions that have yet to be approved, attest to the behavioral and social assumptions made every day in this country. Much of the disparity arises due to the fact that lawmakers are simply not trained in the behavioral and social facts that underlie many of their assumptions and policies written by lawmakers reflect that lack of training. Professionals who are trained in such facts are expected to step up and provide amicus briefs to help limit that disparity.

Questions for Discussion

1. Florida's impact rule has very specific criteria for receiving benefits or compensation. What should the criteria be for receiving benefits or compensation if Florida's definition is inappropriate?

2. a. How do the three opinions of the Florida Fourth District Court of Appeals judges on *Woodard v. Jupiter* (2005) differ with each other? b. Are all three Justices saying the same thing?

3. To what extent was Jeffrey Woodard discriminated against in the school?

4. a. What are the ethical implications of a Bible-based school questioning a student's sexual orientation? b. What are the legal implications of a Bible-based school questioning a student's sexual orientation?

References

Gracey v. Eaker, 837 So.2d 348 (2002).

Hagan v. Coca-Cola Bottling Co., 804 So.2d 1234 (2001).

Kush v. Lloyd, 616 So. 2d 415, 422 (1992).

Wites, M. A.(n.d.). The Florida litigation guide: Emotional distress, negligent infliction. Retrieved December 7, 2007 from http://www.floridalitigationguide.com/guide/21.php

Woodard & Gload v. Jupiter Christian School, Inc. & Bellhorn, 913 So.2d 1188 (2005).

14 MALE VICTIMS OF INTIMATE PARTNER VIOLENCE

Intimate partner violence (IPV) is "physical, sexual, or psychological harm by a current or former partner or spouse" (Centers for Disease Control and Prevention [CDC], 2014, para. 1). Many studies focus specifically on heterosexual relationships with female victims and male perpetrators, but victims of IPV can be women or men in heterosexual or homosexual relationships. Although largely absent in currently available literature, violence against men perpetrated by women in intimate relationships does occur, yet few services are available for male victims of IPV. Further, research has often found that violence against men is seen often as less serious than violence against women perpetrated by men (Harris & Cook, 1994; Seelau & Seelau, 2005; Sorenson & Taylor, 2005). However, the extent to which such abuse occurs is under some debate. Some researchers have argued that the myth of "husband abuse" is nothing more than "feminist backlash," meant to steal power from the women's movement that has made battered wives at the forefront of issues surrounding IPV (Minaker & Snider, 2006). Others have argued that IPV, and domestic violence in general, has historically been perpetrated equally by men *and* women, but movements within the last 40 years have diminished the acknowledgement of men as victims (George, 2007; Hall, 2012). More research is certainly needed, not only to ascertain the true rate of intimate partner victimization of men, but also to understand the experiences of men who are victimized by female partners.

Prevalence of IPV

Since 1994, the overall rate of IPV has declined in the United States. According to information provided through the National Crime

Victimization Survey (NCVS), the rate of IPV declined from 9.8 per 1,000 persons in 1994 to 3.2 per 1,000 persons in 2012. This is a 67% reduction in violence during that time period (Truman & Morgan, 2014). The rates of serious IPV, violence that includes rape, robbery, and aggravated assault, also decreased during that time: 3.6 per 1,000 persons in 1994 to 1.0 per 1,000 persons in 2012. Although the greatest proportion of the reduction of serious violence occurred during the 1990s and early 2000s, serious forms of IPV continued to decline throughout the 2000s (Truman & Morgan, 2014). The reduction of simple assaults by intimate partners followed a similar trend, from 6.2 per 1,000 persons in 1994 to 2.2 per 1,000 persons in 2012 (Truman & Morgan, 2014). In most cases of IPV, the perpetrator was the victim's girl/boyfriend, and women were far more likely to be victims then men (Truman & Morgan, 2014). Although women were more likely to be victims of IPV (and domestic violence overall), both had higher rates of victimization by an intimate partner, for serious violent crimes and simple assaults, than another family member or other relative (Truman & Morgan, 2014).

According to NCVS data from 2003 to 2012, overall, men are far more likely to be victimized by a stranger than someone they know (55% versus 34%). However, men do comprise a sizable portion of reported victimizations: in 24% of all domestic violence victimizations (which includes IPV) and in 18% of intimate partner victimizations from 2003 to 2012, the victim was male. For men victimized by an intimate partner, 13% of the perpetrators were the victims' spouses. In 30% of the cases, the perpetrator was the victim's girl/boyfriend (Truman & Morgan, 2014). Similar to the rates discussed previously, the rates of serious IPV (rape, robbery and aggravated assault) against men declined 64% from 1994 to 2011, from a rate of 1.1 per 1,000 persons to 0.4 per 1,000 persons (Catalano, 2013).

Despite similar trends in victimization, male victims differ from female victims in several ways:

1. Although 39% of IPV experienced by males involved serious forms of violence, approximately 16% of violent victimizations were robberies. Some men have reported sexual assaults, but these reports are relatively rare, and researchers have recommended caution in interpreting the data due to small sample sizes (Catalano, 2013).
2. Men are less likely to be killed by an intimate partner than women; in 2010, men were killed by intimate partners in approximately 3% of cases.
3. Men are more likely than women to be shot at, stabbed, or hit with a weapon (8.2% versus 3.8%) or hit by an object that was held or thrown (19.3% versus 5.4%).

4. Men were more likely to be victimized in the presence of a weapon (27% versus 17.6%; Catalano, 2013).

Women, however, are more likely to sustain serious physical injuries and to be treated for physical injuries resulting from IPV (Catalano, 2013). According to Catalano (2013), even though males are more likely to be victimized by strangers, they experience more serious forms of violence, physical attacks, threats prior to victimization, and injuries when attacked by intimate partners.

Despite the findings reported by the NCVS, some researchers believe the rate of male victimization in intimate relationships is much higher, and that research supports the conclusion that women and men are equal contributors to domestic violence. One such factor that leads to underreports of victimization, according to Hall (2012), is the feminization of the social-welfare system in the United States. Hall (2012) claims that the current social-welfare system is designed to be biased against men; men are only perpetrators of violence because Western patriarchal traditions allow for women only to be victims. Hall (2012) directs attention to the McNeely and Robinson-Simpson (1987) article, which reviewed results of several studies that found women to be as violent as men in domestic violence relationships. These authors claimed studies that contradict preconceived conceptualizations of victims were being ignored, and policies that increased men's "legal and social deafness" were developed continually (p. 485). Some of the same issues concerning the public conceptualization of violence expressed by McNeely and Robinson-Simpson back in 1987 were still problematic, according to Hall, in 2012.

George (2007) claims that the development of the "Rule of Thumb" myth seemingly has directed subsequent IPV research, which has ignored male victims, and has distorted historical information where it is noted that men have always been victims of violence perpetrated by women. "The Rule of Thumb" that is often referenced in domestic violence literature is reportedly an old common law statute that would allow men to beat or "discipline" their wives, as long as the stick was no thicker than his thumb. George (2007) claims, as well as other researchers, that no such statute has ever existed, and that the "Rule of Thumb" is nothing more than a phrase of measure. Historically, men have always been victims of IPV, and their wives have been guilty of such violence (George, 2007).

According to George (2007), society seems to have difficulty accepting the fact that violence against men occurs for two reasons:

1. The myth that men are incapable of being victimized by women.
2. The myth that women are not physically violent or aggressive.

It could be that the second reason is most difficult for society to accept: women are often portrayed as passive, delicate creatures and the images of the physically dominant or sexually aggressive females are difficult to comprehend. Existence of this gender stereotype is often reinforced by studies that examine participant perceptions of men and women in IPV situations.

However, many researchers disagree with the premise that men and women equally perpetrate violently in intimate relationships, or that victimization rates of men are grossly underreported. After the McNeely and Robinson-Simpson (1987) article appeared, Saunders (1988) countered, pointing out the limitations in the research that demonstrated equal likelihood of perpetration: women were using violence because they were acting in self-defense, and many of the studies cited by McNeely and Robinson-Simpson (1987) failed to control for that fact or to take into consideration other gender differences. More recent studies that have considered an increasing number of arrests among women for IPV have found that many of the women arrested were acting in self-defense and were not the primary aggressor (Henning, Renauer, & Holdford, 2006). This finding supports the idea that certain data sources can be misleading, and greater analysis of the sex differences in IPV is warranted.

According to Minaker and Snider (2006), policy changes appear to be taking place in governments and justice systems as the movement towards recognition of "battered husbands" gains attention. The authors claim that such a movement is fueled by feminist backlash, and by the idea that gender equality currently exists, when it so clearly does not. Although battered husbands certainly do exist, and the authors acknowledge that fact, they claim that the degree to which battered husbands have been highlighted in the media and in policy changes is greatly over-inflated as compared to actual rates of occurrence. The damage then becomes apparent in how policies, services, and funding are directed towards programs or research that deal with battered wives. Minaker and Snider (2006) believe that the media and conservative men's groups have led the movement towards an idea of equal battering across the sexes, although research indicates clearly that women are more likely to be victims of domestic violence, and their injuries tend to be more serious.

Minaker and Snider (2006) also suggest that the language that has been newly adopted by policymakers diminishes the fact that women experience IPV more often than men, having moved from language of "wife-battering" to that of "domestic violence." What the authors have failed to acknowledge, however, is that such gender-specific wording in statute greatly diminishes men's needs within the system and ignores same-sex couples. From a policy perspective, neutrality is best.

Perception of Male Victimization

Regardless of the debate over prevalence, violence against men by women in intimate relationships does occur; however, individuals may not perceive male victimization to be as serious as female victimization. Sorenson and Taylor (2005) studied assailant gender on community perceptions of IPV situations; 3,679 California participants were given vignettes describing a scenario of IPV and then asked a series of questions regarding whether the participant believed the assailant's behavior was wrong, illegal, or both, and what should happen to the assailant and the victim. Researchers found that male assailants were judged more harshly than female assailants. Sorenson and Taylor (2005) also found that participants were less likely to find the females' actions to be wrong, illegal, or both, and were less likely to believe that the male victims needed some form of intervention, such as police involvement, restraining orders, or both.

Seelau and Seelau (2005) studied perceptions of heterosexual and homosexual domestic violence relationships with 192 undergraduate students, who were asked to read a summary of a domestic violence scenario and to answer several questions. Four possible conditions existed: male-to-female violence, male-to-male violence, female-to-male violence, and female-to-female violence. All participants found the scenarios to be relatively serious, but scenarios involving female victims were found to be more serious, with female victims of male assailants being the most serious (Seelau & Seelau, 2005). Participants were more likely to indicate the need for a citation or arrest for scenarios involving female victims, but only warnings for scenarios involving female perpetrators. Overall, Seelau & Seelau (2005) found that participants assumed that female victims suffered from more serious injuries. Also, participants were more likely to issue guilty verdicts to male perpetrators.

In a Harris & Cook (1994) study involving 372 college students, participants were given one of three scenarios that described an incident of IPV: a husband battering his wife, a wife battering her husband, or a gay male battering his partner. Some of the scenarios also included verbal provocation by the victim. As compared to male participants, female participants

- found the scenarios to be more violent,
- indicated that they would be more willing to call the police if they had witnessed the event,
- found the batterer to be more responsible,
- liked the victim more, and
- believed that the victim should leave the batterer (Harris & Cook, 1994).

Overall, participants found the wife-battering scenario to be more violent, and would be more likely to call the police in that situation, than if the victim was the husband or partner. Husbands were found to be more responsible for the battering than wives, as victims or perpetrators, and participants also believe that they should be convicted more than the wives. Participants liked the wife victim the most and the gay victim the least (Harris & Cook, 1994). Lehmann and Santilli (1996) also found that participants tend to blame male victims more for their abuse than female victims.

Female Aggression

Researchers have found that women can be just as aggressive as, or even more aggressive than, men in intimate relationships. Women tend to be more aggressive towards family members and intimate partners, whereas, men are more likely to target that aggression against those outside of the family. Even though women may be more aggressive in intimate partner relationships, aggression towards women by men tends to result in serious injury more often than aggression towards men by women (Biller, 1995; Graham-Kevan, 2007). Cross, Tee, and Campbell (2011) found that women tend to be more aggressive towards intimate partners because of the intimacy of the relationships, while men tend to decrease their level of aggression in intimate relationships because of their partner's gender. In a study of female college freshman, Testa, Hoffman, and Leonard (2011) found that participants reported perpetrating more physical and psychological aggression than their male partners. In fact, most participants reported participating in mutually aggressive relationships, and when asymmetrical aggression did occur, it was most often coming from females. Apart from physical aggression, Carroll and colleagues (2010) reported that women tend to use relational aggression, such as intentionally ignoring a spouse, withholding sex, or embarrassing a spouse in front of others, more often than men in marriages.

Characteristics of Male Victims

Characteristics and experiences of male victims of IPV are not widely available, but one of the first studies to report comprehensive information on male victims was conducted by Hines, Brown, and Dunning (2007). Their analysis included information on 190 men, who, on their own behalf, had called the Domestic Abuse Helpline for Men (DAHM) between January of 2002 and November of 2003 (Hines et al., 2007). Most of the callers had learned of the helpline through its website or from media reports. The mean age of callers was 41.32, ranging from 19 to 64 years old. The mean age of female partners was 35.98, ranging from 17 to 59 years old. 52.1% were currently in an abusive relationship, and 56.3% reported having children in the home, ranging from 1 to 23 years old (Hines et al., 2007).

Reported occupations included everything from police, fire, and military to medical, legal, and other professional occupations. Some were not able to divulge their occupations without revealing their identity, suggesting high-profile employment; 27.4% were either unemployed or disabled. Although not all callers answered all questions posed by helpline volunteers, most reported acts of physical violence, stalking, or both, including slapping, pushing, kicking, choking, being spat on, scratching, and stabbing (Hines et al., 2007). Some callers also reported attacks or threats of attacks to the genitals. A majority of them also reported controlling behaviors, including threats and coercion, emotional abuse, and intimidation. The intimidation included threats to withhold custody of children, calling the police to report false incidents of violence by the victim, and destroying items around the house (Hines et al., 2007).

Some callers described the manipulations their wives or female partners had pulled on the domestic violence system. Male victims could be taken into custody for false allegations reported by partners, receive restraining orders, be denied access to children, or ordered/referred into batterers' programs. Clearly, male victims are re-victimized by the system: follow-up calls to agencies by DAHM staff often corroborated accounts provided by callers. Other agencies would dismiss male victims' reports, often assuming they were the batterers in the relationship (Hines et al., 2007). Hines and colleagues (2007) also collected data on perpetrators from the victims and found that 91.7% had a history of childhood trauma, 61.9% had threatened suicide, 59% had threatened homicide, 52.1% used alcohol, 46% had a mental illness, and 34.8% used drugs.

In a later study to examine help-seeking behaviors, Douglas and Hines (2011) reported that men who sought help often used informal types of support, such as friends and family, and were most satisfied with this type of support. About half of the study participants also sought assistance from local domestic violence agencies and police departments, but they generally found them unsupportive. Participants reported that domestic violence agencies often would turn them away or accuse them of actually being the batterers. Interactions with police were similar; participants reported that police often disregarded the violence as serious because victims were men, who in their mind, should be able to protect themselves (Douglas & Hines, 2011). This victim blaming or victim shaming may certainly influence the likelihood of help-seeking behavior among male victims.

Conclusion

The actual rate of male victimization by female intimate partners has been debated for some time; data from the NCVS suggests that male victimizations from IPV is decreasing and is considerably less than women victimizations. However, some researchers believe that incidents are underreported, and that male victimization is nearly equal to that of female victimization. Others believe that data fails to support the hypothesis of equivalency in intimate partner victimization, and over-emphasis of male victimization distracts from the violence experienced by women, perpetrated by men. The public certainly perceives violence against women as being more serious, and this perception can lead to both disproportionate access to services and revictimization by service providers.

Only recently has the true nature of male victimization begun to be explored by researchers, and far more research is needed to understand the unique experiences of men victimized by their female intimate partners. As suggested by Hines and Douglas (2009), the discussion needs to move away from who perpetrates or suffers from IPV most often. Ideally, the focus should be on understanding victimization in general and learning how to best meet the needs of victims, regardless of their gender.

Questions for Discussion

1. Is the prevalence of victimization of males by intimate partners sufficient to warrant concern by law enforcement, government officials or the general population?

2. Could the existence of or increase in male victimization by intimate partners be the result of a public campaign focusing on male violence, such as teaching boys not to hit girls?

3. To what extent does the change in name from "wife-battering" to "domestic violence" actually create a sense that men can be battered just as easily as women?

4. From the perspective of law enforcement, how is the plight of female victims diminished by a concern over male victims of intimate partner violence? To what extent should law enforcement be concerned with the plight of male victims?

References

Biller, H.B. (1995). The battered spouse may be male. *Brown University Child & Adolescent Behavior Letter, 11*(3), 1-2.

Carroll, J.S., Nelson, D.A., Yorgason, J.B., Harper, J.M., Hagmann Ashton, R., & Jensen, A.C. (2010). Relational aggression in marriage. *Aggressive Behavior, 36*, 315-329.

Catalano, S. (2013). Intimate partner violence: Attributes of victimization, 1993-2011 (NCJ 243300). Retrieved from Bureau of Justice Statistics website: http://www.bjs.gov/ index.cfm?ty=pbdetail&iid=4801

Centers for Disease Control and Prevention. (2014). Intimate partner violence: Definitions. Retrieved from http://www.cdc.gov/violenceprevention/intimatepartnerviolence/

definitions.html

Cross, C.P., Tee, W., & Campbell, A. (2011). Gender symmetry in intimate aggression: An effect of intimacy or target sex? *Aggressive Behavior, 37*, 268-277.

Douglas, E.M., & Hines, D.A. (2011). The helpseeking experiences of men who sustain intimate partner violence: An overlooked population and implications for practice. *Journal of Family Violence, 26*, 473-485.

George, M.J. (2007). The "Great Taboo" and the role of patriarchy in husband and wife abuse. *International Journal of Men's Health, 6*(1), 7-21.

Graham-Kevan, N. (2007). The re-emergence of male victims. *International Journal of Men's Health, 6*(1), 3-6.

Hall, R.E. (2012). The feminization of social welfare: Implications of cultural tradition vis-à-vis male victims of domestic violence. *Journal of Sociology & Social Welfare, 39*(3), 7-27.

Harris, R.J. & Cook, C.A. (1994). Attributions about spouse abuse: It matters who the batterers and victims are. *Sex Roles, 30*(7/8), 553-565.

Henning, K., Renauer, B., & Holdford, R. (2006). Victim or offender? Heterogeneity among women arrested for intimate partner violence. *Journal of Family Violence, 21*, 351-368.

Hines, D.A., Brown, J., & Dunning, E. (2007). Characteristics of callers to the Domestic Abuse Helpline for Men. *Journal of Family Violence, 22*, 63-72.

Hines, D.A., & Douglas, E.M. (2009). Women's use of intimate partner violence against men: Prevalence, implications, and consequences. *Journal of Aggression, Maltreatment & Trauma, 18*, 572-586.

Lehmann, M., & Santilli, N.R. (1996). Sex differences in perceptions of spousal abuse. *Journal of Social Behavior and Personality, 11*(5), 229-238.

McNeely, R.L., & Robinson-Simpson, G. (1987). The truth about domestic violence: A falsely framed issue. *Social Work, 32*(6), 485-490.

Minaker, J.C. & Snider, L. (2006). Husband abuse: Equality with a vengeance? *Canadian Journal of Criminology and Criminal Justice, 48*(5), 753-780.

Seelau, S., & Seelau, E. (2005). Gender-role stereotypes and perceptions of heterosexual, gay and lesbian domestic violence. *Journal of Family Violence 20*(6), 363-371. doi: 10.1007/s10896-005-7798-4

Saunders, D.G. (1988). Other "truths" about domestic violence: A reply to McNeely and Robinson-Simpson. *Social Work, 33*(2), 179-183.

Sorenson, S.B. & Taylor, C.A. (2005). Female aggression toward male intimate partners: An examination of social norms in a community-based sample. *Psychology of Women Quarterly, 29*, 78-96.

Testa, M., Hoffman, J.H., & Leonard, K.E. (2011). Female intimate partner violence perpetration: Stability and predictors of mutual and nonmetal aggression across the first year of college. *Aggressive Behavior, 37*, 362-373.

Truman, J.L., & Morgan, R.E. (2014). Nonfatal domestic violence, 2003-2012 (NCJ 244697). Retrieved from Bureau of Justice Statistics website: http://www.bjs.gov/index.cfm?ty= pbdetail&iid=4984

APPENDIX

SELECT CONSTITUTIONAL AMENDMENTS OF INTEREST IN FORENSIC PSYCHOLOGY

First Amendment
Congress shall make no law respecting an establishment of religion, or prohibiting the free exercise thereof; or abridging the freedom of speech, or of the press, or the right of the people peaceably to assemble, and to petition the Government for a redress of grievances.

Second Amendment
A well regulated Militia, being necessary to the security of a free State, the right of the people to keep and bear Arms, shall not be infringed.

Third Amendment
No Soldier shall, in time of peace be quartered in any house, without the consent of the Owner, nor in time of war, but in a manner to be prescribed by law.

Fourth Amendment
The right of the people to be secure in their persons, houses, papers, and effects, against unreasonable searches and seizures, shall not be violated, and no Warrants shall issue, but upon probable cause, supported by Oath or affirmation, and particularly describing the place to be searched, and the persons or things to be seized.

Fifth Amendment
No person shall be held to answer for a capital, or otherwise infamous crime, unless on a presentment or indictment of a Grand Jury, except in cases arising in the land or naval forces, or in the Militia, when in actual service in time of War or public danger; nor shall any person be subject for the same offence to be twice put in jeopardy of life or limb, nor shall be compelled in any criminal case to be a witness against himself, nor be deprived of life, liberty, or property, without due process of law; nor shall private property be taken for public use without just compensation.

Sixth Amendment

In all criminal prosecutions, the accused shall enjoy the right to a speedy and public trial, by an impartial jury of the State and district wherein the crime shall have been committed; which district shall have been previously ascertained by law, and to be informed of the nature and cause of the accusation; to be confronted with the witnesses against him; to have compulsory process for obtaining witnesses in his favor, and to have the assistance of counsel for his defence.

Seventh Amendment

In Suits at common law, where the value in controversy shall exceed twenty dollars, the right of trial by jury shall be preserved, and no fact tried by a jury shall be otherwise re-examined in any Court of the United States, than according to the rules of the common law.

Eighth Amendment

Excessive bail shall not be required, nor excessive fines imposed, nor cruel and unusual punishments inflicted.

Ninth Amendment

The enumeration in the Constitution of certain rights shall not be construed to deny or disparage others retained by the people.

Tenth Amendment

The powers not delegated to the United States by the Constitution, nor prohibited by it to the States, are reserved to the States respectively, or to the people.

Fourteenth Amendment

§ 1. All persons born or naturalized in the United States, and subject to the jurisdiction thereof, are citizens of the United States and of the State wherein they reside. No State shall make or enforce any law which shall abridge the privileges or immunities of citizens of the United States; nor shall any State deprive any person of life, liberty, or property, without due process of law; nor deny to any person within its jurisdiction the equal protection of the laws.

§ 2. Representatives shall be apportioned among the several States according to their respective numbers, counting the whole number of persons in each State, excluding Indians not taxed. But when the right to vote at any election for the choice of electors for President and Vice President of the United States, Representatives in Congress, the Executive and judicial officers of a State, or the members of the Legislature thereof, is denied to any of the male inhabitants of such State, being twenty-one years of age, and citizens of the United States, or in any way abridged, except for participation in rebellion, or other crime, the basis of representation therein shall be reduced in the proportion which the number of such male citizens shall bear to the whole number of male citizens twenty-one years of age in such State.

§ 3. No person shall be a Senator or Representative in Congress, or elector of President and Vice President, or hold any office, civil or military, under the United States, or under any State, who, having previously taken an oath, as a member of Congress, or as an officer of the United States, or as a member of any State legislature, or as an executive or judicial officer of any State, to support the Constitution of the United States, shall have engaged in insurrection or rebellion against the same, or given aid or comfort to the enemies thereof. But Congress may by a vote of two-thirds of each House, remove such disability.

§ 4. The validity of the public debt of the United States, authorized by law, including debts incurred for payment of pensions and bounties for services in suppressing insurrection or rebellion, shall not be questioned. But neither the United States nor any State shall assume or pay any debt or obligation incurred in aid of insurrection or rebellion against the United States, or any claim for the loss or emancipation of any slave; but all such debts, obligations and claims shall be held illegal and void.

§ 5. The Congress shall have power to enforce, by appropriate legislation, the provisions of this article.

GLOSSARY

ACLU   American Civil Liberties Union

ADHD   Attention-Deficit Hyperactivity Disorder

administrative model   A decision-making model where decision makers look for the first solution that is good enough to remedy a problem without looking for the best solution to a problem

ambiguity theory   A decision-making model where there is not enough information to establish a personal belief system so the decisions that are made are based on an ever-changing vantage point

American Civil Liberties Union   A non-profit organization whose mission is to defend the Constitutional rights of all Americans

American Psychiatric Association   An organization of psychiatrists who publish the Diagnostic and Statistical Manual of Mental Disorders and work to ensure humane care and effective treatment for individuals with mental illness

APA   American Psychological Association

APA Division 30   American Psychological Association's Society of Psychological Hypnosis

attitudinal model   A decision-making model that proposes that, if a behavior does not match the judge's ideology, attitudes, or values, then the judge will rule against the behavior

auditory information   Recordings and information that is experienced only through the sense of hearing

aversion therapy   A behavioral therapy technique in which a person eliminates an undesired behavior by learning to associate the behavior with discomfort

behavioral assumption Beliefs about human behavior that may or may not be supported by observable facts; the premise of faulty decisions made within the legal system

behavioral therapies A collection of therapies based upon the belief that all behavior is learned; the goal of behavioral therapy is to teach new ways of behaving

big brother A colloquial term referring to the watchful eye of the government

California's Sexually Violent Predator Act Civil legislation passed in California in 1995 to identify, contain, and rehabilitate the most violent sexual offenders

California Summary Parole Initiative A California State policy proposal that was meant to release non-violent, non-serious, and non-sex offenders who had served most of their sentences behind prison walls a up to 20 months before they completed their sentences

CASOMB California Sex Offender Management Board

CDCR California Department of Corrections and Rehabilitation

CDMH California Department of Mental Health

CDC Centers for Disease Control and Prevention

CHPQ Chronic Health Problems Questionnaire

civil commitment Institutional detention, usually within a State run mental hospital of an individual after he or she serves his or her sentence; the purpose of which is to prevent future offending

civil liability An individual may be responsible for an aspect of civil law or in violation of some aspect of civil law

civil penalties Punishments for civil offenses such as fines or short incarceration

cognitive interview   An interviewing technique used with eyewitnesses and victims of crime to enhance memory recall in which witnesses are instructed to recreate the incident in their minds and questioning is more open-ended and witness-directed

cognitive model   A decision-making model where problem-solving activities are used resulting in the selection of a belief or a course of action among several alternative possibilities

color of the law   The appearance that legal right or authority to perform an act exists when it does not

common law   A branch of law that is not codified but rather relies on judges to make reasonable and informed decisions about cases

community policing   A form of policing where law enforcement agency personnel solicit assistance from members of the community or neighborhood

context reinstatement   Recreating a context in which an event occurred in order to enhance memory recall

continuity of care   The continuation and maintenance of an adequate level of physical and mental health care

correctional psychology   A subfield of forensic psychology concerned with the application of psychological principles to all aspects of the correctional system

counter-conditioning   A technique in which an undesired response to a stimulus is replaced by a new response to the same stimulus

CPTSD   Complex Post-Traumatic Stress Disorder

criminal penalties   Punishments for criminal offenses such as prison incarceration or capital punishment

criminal psychology   A subfield of forensic psychology concerned with psychological theories of crime and their application to the justice system

culpability The responsibility or blameworthiness of an individual; usually an offender

DAHM Domestic Abuse Helpline for Men

descriptive decision making A psychological decision making strategy that attempts to discern how people actually make decision while taking people and circumstances into account

diathesis stress model A theory in psychology that posits that stress experienced exposes a predisposed vulnerability to some behavior resulting in the manifestation of that behavior

DSM Diagnostic and Statistical Manual of Mental Disorders

Electronic Communications Privacy Act A Federal policy initiative created with the purpose of expanding government restrictions on wiretaps beyond telephone calls to computer-based information

electronic surveillance A method of monitoring a home, business, or individual using a variety of audio and visual recording devices

emotional distress Psychological agony experienced as a result of a severe or traumatic event

Family Therapy A form of group therapy that is based upon the theory that the family structure impacts individual behavior

FBI Federal Bureau of Investigation

feature-intensive processing decision making A decision-making model that focuses on the specific costs and benefits of engaging in a given activity

Florida's impact rule A Florida common law requirement that allows for payment to be made to the victim of emotional distress only when some physical injury occurred in conjunction to the emotional distress

focused meditation A technique to enhance memory recall for an event; similar to hypnosis

forensic hypnosis   The utilization of hypnosis in the field of criminal justice to uncover or remember unconscious or subconscious details about a crime

forensic hypnotic interviewing   The use of hypnotic interviewing techniques in a forensic setting

forensic psychology   The application of psychological concepts to issues and problems in the justice system

GAS   General Adaptation Syndrome

gestalt decision making   A decision-making model that is characterized by a failure to thoroughly consider the costs and benefits of a given activity

GPS   Global Positioning System

gross stress reaction   An antiquated term used in the first edition of the DSM; a stress syndrome that was a response to an exceptional physical or mental stress

high-profile crimes   Crimes that attract considerable attention and interest from the media and the public

Hippocratic Oath   An ethical and philosophical perspective head by members of the healthcare profession based on the concept of doing no harm

human smuggling   A business transaction between willing parties involving the movement across an international border in violation of the laws

human trafficking   The exploitation of persons through force, or the threat of force, coercion, deception, and manipulation

hypnosis   A state of consciousness in which a person is highly susceptible to suggestion or direction and is characterized by intense focus and decreased awareness of peripheral events

hypnotic hypermnesia   Memory retrieval or enhancement through hypnosis

hypnotically aided testimony The recollection of subconscious memories about events surrounding a crime which is given to authorities while under hypnosis and can be considered part of the individual's testimony in court; often used interchangeably with *hypnotically enhanced testimony* or *hypnotically refreshed testimony*

hypnotically enhanced testimony The recollection of subconscious memories about events surrounding a crime which is given to authorities while under hypnosis and can be considered part of the individual's testimony in court; often used interchangeably with *hypnotically aided testimony* or *hypnotically refreshed testimony*

hypnotically refreshed testimony The recollection of subconscious memories about events surrounding a crime which is given to authorities while under hypnosis and can be considered part of the individual's testimony in court; often used interchangeably with *hypnotically aided testimony* or *hypnotically enhanced testimony*

impact rule A Florida State legal standard that requires any emotional distress suffered stem from the physical injuries caused by an impact before recovery of damages could be awarded to the plaintiff

incremental model A decision-making model that utilizes multiple levels of comparison in order to come to a final conclusion, thereby reducing the number of possible solution alternatives

intelligence-gathering techniques An overarching term used to describe the process of collecting and preserving information about individuals

intimate partner violence A physical, sexual, or psychological harm committed by a current or former partner or spouse

IPV Intimate Partner Violence

irritable heart A precursor to Post-Traumatic Stress Disorder; a term given to individuals during the mid-19th century to describe a physiological reaction to participating in combat post-Civil War

Jacob Wetterling Crimes Against Children and Sexually Violent Offender Registration Act   Federal legislation that required each state to create a registry for offenders convicted of sexual offenses and certain other offenses against children

Jessica's Law   A Florida law requiring all individuals convicted of a sexual offense against a child be given a minimum of 25 years in prison

law school model   A decision-making model where the facts and issues in a case are assessed and then compared to precedent, applicable laws, and state and Federal Constitutional law

legal psychology   A subfield of forensic psychology concerned with the application of psychological principles to all aspects of the court system including prosecutors, defense attorneys and juries

MDSO   Mentally disordered sexual offender

Megan's Law   A Federal law that requires law enforcement agencies to publically disclose details about sexual offenses and the offenders convicted of the offenses

mixed scanning model   A decision-making model where individuals make incremental changes, using solutions that are just good enough, in the hopes that those incremental changes will eventually lead to the best solution

NCVS   National Crime Victimization Survey

normative decision making   An idealistic decision making strategy that addresses how decision ought to be made apart from observations of people or circumstances

occupational stress   A biological and psychological reaction to unfavorable events in the workplace

PCL   PTSD Checklist; A 17-item self-report measure to examine symptoms of Post-Traumatic Stress Disorder

perceptual shorthand   A method of making decisions based on one's past experiences and best guesses about the circumstances of the situation

police and investigative psychology   A subfield of forensic psychology concerned with the application of psychological principles to all aspects of law enforcement including interrogation

Post-Traumatic Stress Disorder   A formal psychological diagnosis; a psychological disorder resulting from surviving shocking, terrifying or life-threatening events

PQ   Prostitution Questionnaire

pre-hypnotic testimony   The recollection of subconscious memories about events surrounding a crime which is given to authorities prior to being hypnotized

pre-release planning   The process by which incarcerated individuals gain assistance with preparing for and transitioning to life outside the correctional facility

preventative detention   Imprisonment that is used to prevent future offending rather than as a punishment

Proposition 83   An initiated state statute approved by California voters in 2006 that required GPS monitoring and residency restrictions for registered sex offenders; Also known as Jessica's Law

prospect theory   A decision-making model where decisions are based on probabilities of a certain result from one perspective – failing to take into account all situations, outcomes, and consequences

PTSD   Post-Traumatic Stress Disorder

Public Safety Realignment Initiative   An improvement on the California Summary Parole Initiative where custody and control of non-violent, non-serious, and non-sex offenders was transferred to county governments

Railway Spine Syndrome   An early variation of Post-Traumatic Stress Disorder that described the patient's symptoms as a result of having been involved in a spine-injuring train accident

realignment initiative   A restructuring of the California parole system whereby inmates released would be supervised by county agencies rather than the state agency

Reality Therapy   A therapeutic technique based on Choice Theory in which individuals learn to be more aware of their choices and how their choices impact their goals

re-entry facility   A community based facility in which previously incarcerated individuals can transition from prison life to life back in the community

rehabilitative programs   A set of physical and psychological interventions aimed at restoring convicted individuals to functioning members of society following their incarceration

reinforcement   The strengthening or weakening of behavior by using rewards or punishments

"Rule of Thumb"   Alleged common law statute that would allow men to beat or "discipline" their wives, as long as the stick was no thicker than his thumb

schema theory   A decision-making model that emphasizes the acquisition of new data in order to integrate it into a decision makers pre-existing belief system

sex offender   A individual convicted of a sex offense

sexual psychopath   A legal term that describes behavior characterized by illegal or socially unacceptable sexual aggressiveness, as well as by a lack of regard for the feelings of the sexual partner under duress

sexual psychopath laws   Early sex offender management legislation that established guidelines for the civil commitment of sexual offenders who had committed their crimes due to an underlying psychiatric disease or psychopathic personality

sexually violent predator   A person charged with or convicted of a sexually violent offense, such as rape

shell shock   An early variation of Post-Traumatic Stress Disorder whereby the patient was believed to have suffered from tiny sections of exploded bombs lodging themselves in the patient's brain

social learning theory   A theory of crime whereby behavior of inferior members of a group is learned from superior members of the group

Society of Psychological Hypnosis   Division 30 of the American Psychological Association dedicated to the study, teaching, and practice of hypnosis

soldier's heart   A precursor to Post-Traumatic Stress Disorder; a term given to individuals during the mid-19th century to describe a physiological reaction to participating in combat post-Civil War

summary parole   The release of incarcerated inmates classified as non-violent, non-serious, and non-sex offenders before the entirety of their sentence is served

SVP   Sexually Violent Predator

therapeutic hypnosis   Also known as hypnotherapy; the use of hypnosis in medical or psychological treatment

three-drug cocktail   A method of lethal injection commonly used by states to carry out capital punishment; the three drugs typically include a sedative, a paralytic agent and a drug to induce cardiac arrest

Title 42 U.S. Code Section 1983   A United States law which allows for a legal means of protecting all constitutional rights

transient situation disturbance   An antiquated term used in the second edition of the DSM; a stress syndrome that was a response to an exceptional physical or mental stress

vicarious liability   A government agency is responsible for the individuals it employs

victim blaming   A concept of victimology that places responsibility for a crime partially or entirely on the victim of the crime

victim shaming   A concept of victimology similar to that of victim blaming whereby the victim is partially or entirely blamed for bringing the crime upon himself or herself and shamed because of his or her victimization

victimless crime   A crime where the assumption that there is no victim is made because the individual participates in the legal or illegal activity of his or her own choice

victimology   A subfield of forensic psychology concerned with the application of psychological principles to understand the plight of victims and assist in their restoration after victimization

video policing   A force-multiplying strategy to enforce laws in a particular area by utilizing video cameras and video recording devices

video surveillance   The usage of video and audio recording devices to monitor individuals' movements

visual information   Recordings and information that is experienced through the sense of vision

Washington Community Protection Act of 1990   The first comprehensive set of laws regarding the management of sexual offenders passed in the United States; legislation that created provisions for the punishment and treatment of sexual offenders, compensation for victims, and civil commitment of sexual predators

INDEX

U.S. Supreme Court, 3, 4, 18, 19,
54, 76, 81, 82, 89, 90, 91, 92,
93, 99, 100, 101, 102, 103, 104,
105, 106, 107, 108, 115, 116,
118, 121, 122
U.S. v. Halper., 3
unconstitutional, 17, 87, 91, 92,
103, 106
United States v. Salerno, 91
United States v. Torres, 72, 78, 79
United States v. Ursery, 93, 96

vicarious liability, 20, 150
victim blaming, 133, 150, 151

victim shaming, 133, 151
victimless crime, 28, 33, 151
video policing, 3, 71, 76, 78, 151
video surveillance, 71, 72, 73, 74,
75, 76, 77, 78, 79, 151
visual information, 72, 151
Vitek v. Jones, 81

Washington Community
Protection Act, 86, 96, 151
Woodard v. Jupiter, 121, 122, 126

Zinermon v. Burch, 81

ABOUT THE AUTHORS

Jared Linebach received his Ph.D. from the California School of Forensic Studies in 2011 in forensic psychology. His accomplishments include several works including *Nonparametric Statistics for Applied Research* (2013) published by Springer Science+Business Media New York. His main research interest is in campus law enforcement. Jared also works with doctoral candidates regarding their methodological and statistical approaches to research.

Lea Kovacsiss received her Ph.D. from the California School of Forensic Studies in 2011 in forensic psychology. Her accomplishments include *Nonparametric Statistics for Applied Research* (2013) published by Springer Science+Business Media New York. Lea currently works in law enforcement as a research analyst. Her research interests include child victims of homicide and criminal justice policy and law.

CPSIA information can be obtained
at www.ICGtesting.com
Printed in the USA
LVOW13s1110220518
578074LV00005B/611/P